EXPLORING
THE LAKE DISTRICT

100 YEARS AGO

EXPLORING

THE LAKE DISTRICT

100 YEARS AGO

SELECTED AND EDITED BY

STUART D. LUDLUM

THAMES AND HUDSON

OTHER TITLES IN THIS SERIES

EXPLORING CORNWALL
100 YEARS AGO

EXPLORING THE WILD WELSH COAST
100 YEARS AGO

EXPLORING SHAKESPEARE COUNTRY
100 YEARS AGO

Original articles by Moncure D. Conway first published in *Harper's New Monthly Magazine* in 1880/81

This edition first published in Great Britain in 1985 by Thames and Hudson Ltd, London

Printed and bound in Great Britain by Butler & Tanner Ltd, Frome and London

FRONT COVER: HELVELLYN AND THIRLMERE

LAKES AND FELLS AND POETS

THE unparalleled beauty of England's Lake District was as seductive to the traveller of the 1880s as it is today. The craggy fells are as majestic as any artist could imagine, the valleys as green and fertile, the mountain streams as clear and scintillating, the lakes themselves—from the great expanse of Windermere to the smallest of the tarns—as varied in their moods and colourings. This is a magical, many-textured landscape, now fierce, now gentle, still to a large extent untamed, spoilt only here and there by the interfering hand, or the obtrusive presence, of man.

It is small wonder that such natural enchantment should have inspired some of England's most sensitive spirits: Coleridge, Southey, De Quincey, but always foremost among them the incomparable Wordsworth—the very personification of Lakeland. His memory is everywhere: on the school desk on which he carved his name at Hawkshead, at Dove Cottage and Rydal Mount, and on the simple gravestone in Grasmere's churchyard. These were places of pilgrimage a century ago for tourists of a literary turn of mind, and so they are today.

In this more hectic, less impressionable age, the modern visitor may be surprised to find how much remains the same. While the swan-maidens of Belle Isle may now be a rarer species, a moonlight row on Windermere still holds the same romance, and fresh-grilled char from its depths tastes no less delicious. Coniston continues to welcome its share of honeymooners, and 'The Mortal Man' at Troutbeck to refresh the thirsty walker. Every July, Ambleside observes its rush-bearing ceremony; each August, Grasmere holds its sports.

So much remains familiar that it may be hard to realize that a hundred years and more have passed since this engaging account was written. Such is the potency of Lakeland's unique allure.

WINDERMERE.

IN the midwinter of an exceptionally dismal and unhappy year for England, the writer hereof was one of a company assembled in the studio of an eminent artist in London to listen to an essay written and read by a young literary lady. The company numbered about sixty, and consisted chiefly of poets, artists, and literary critics. The subject selected by our essayist was the old poem "Tristan," by Gottfried von Strasburg. The authoress by finest artistic touches brought before us the simple pathos and sweetness of that most passionate of mediæval love stories, and with learning treated comparatively the variations of a legend found in many regions, each of which now claims to have originated it. What a picture did old Gottfried bring before us of the enchanted valley to which the hapless Queen Iseult and her lover wandered when driven forth from the palace of the King of Cornwall! A valley green and flower-gemmed, with every tree pleasant for shade or fruit; there is a grove of olive-trees in which nightingales sing, and a wondrous fountain leaping to a diamond-tree in the sunshine, and singing in the moonlight, which seems never to wane for the lovers—who dwell there three years in a grot beauti-

Wm Wordsworth

ful enough to have been sculptured for fairies.

For our little assembly in Fitzroy Square this dream of beauty had the background of the most dark and dismal winter known under the reign of Victoria. Snows, rains, fogs, and freezing winds had persisted through months in giving some physical corollary to a moral season of frauds and failures, depression in trade, and consequent strikes and starvation, miserable wars upon foreign tribes, and angry political discords at home. As against this blackness was set the picture of the olive grove and nightingales, the fountain, flowers, and fairy grot, with even the side suggestion of a genial climate in Iseult's single garment, "through which her limbs were displayed as much as was seemly," one might almost have expected that the poetic and artistic company would rise up with a determination to adjourn in a body to some southern land where the citron blooms, and the orange lights up the leafy glooms. But mark what followed. No sooner was the delightful paper concluded than the comments and criticisms of those present began. The main question raised

was as to the country in which the legend originated; and what was my surprise to find nearly all claiming it as a purely British-Celt poem! There might be a question whether it were an Irish, Scotch, or Cornish legend; but not even the olive-trees seemed to stagger the general conviction that the paradise was evolved on these islands, and the philtre surviving in the penny love-drops still bought by Highland lassies in remote districts. One scholar present ventured to suggest an Oriental origin, but no one seconded him. As for myself, I sat silent. I thought I knew the far region of fairy grots and fountains, but would not mention it, for it was with an admiration akin to awe that I witnessed the simple faith of these cultured gentlemen and ladies in the paradisaic resources of their country. I had no heart to express my misgivings that the three sweet years of the lovers would have been cut short in any British valley where they might attempt to dwell in such a primitive way; that there are only a few mud-holes called caves in this country, which it would require extra fairy-power to transform into lovers' grots; that the leaping fountain would have to be reversed and made to fall from the sky before it could resemble anything known to the British landscape. What is all that scenery compared with the power of the poetic imagination to see it where it does not exist? Here was a pleasant illustration of the especial character of the English poet; the intensity of his inner life; his power of second-sight, so to say, and of seeing his picture under a light that never was on sea or land. The beautiful scenery of Great Britain has been so largely evolved out of the inner consciousness of poets that it would be an interesting experiment to take an imaginative American on a tour of the English lakes under an impression that he was travelling in Wales. The American who has seen the best mountain and lake scenery of his own country might pronounce the Welsh scenery more grand than that of the English lakes; that is, supposing he could see the two as so much combination of land and water; but that he can not do: he must see these English lakes as exalted and spiritualized in a poetic mirage. Never again can one look upon mere Rydal Water; he must see therein the reflected vault of

of a week will have to let some sunshine through when one is wandering after the zigzag track of cheery Christopher North.

The scenery is all picturesque, and sometimes sublime. But its chief charm of decoration is that which the poets have given it. One finds not here the quaint white turrets lanced from the river-side hills of France, or the graceful chalets which give an air of culture to the Italian lakes. Art has done nothing for the English lakes, and, I am sorry to say, Religion has done rather worse, in surrounding some of them with remarkably ugly churches--the ugliest, perhaps, being that at Ambleside, of which Harriet Martineau wrote, "There have been various reductions of the beauty of the valley within twenty years or so; but this is the worst, because the most conspicuous." The weather is rarely beautiful, and "seeing the lakes" sometimes means glimpsing lunettes between the points of an umbrella. Here are no peasants dancing in gay dresses, nor merry fairs surviving from that mythical realm, "merrie old England." The traveller finds here beautiful Nature unadorned but not inanimate; through reverent genius a subtle life-giving breath

SEEING THE LAKES.

Wordsworth's pure reason. Nevermore will Lodore dash down its flood and foam save with the rhythm of Southey. East winds will not bite so keen as we pass through the woodland where Felicia Hemans found repose; and the pelting storm

has gone abroad, and invested hill, dale, and lake with mystical groves and grots and fountains, beside which even the enchanted valley of Tristan is somewhat theatrical.

The train from London touches the

9

Lake District first at Windermere. The village that begins to bear that name is a recent accretion around the station. The knowing traveller does not stop there, but at Bowness, where he finds the hotel "Old England," which more than merits its name. Its beautiful garden slopes to the waters of Windermere, and one may there eat the finest fish of the country—or what he will think such just after travelling from London—the "char," while watching the fisherman with his sail, who is netting the next. Agassiz identified this strange fish, found in five of these lakes, and nowhere else in the country, with the *Ombre chevalier* of Lake Geneva, and it is surmised that the Romans introduced it into these waters. If so, there are few Roman remains which the traveller will find so interesting in this region as this pretty foot-long char, with its golden flesh beneath silvery raiment. Why it is called a "char" I can not say, unless it be that like chores and char-women it comes round at a certain time.

There are other things also found at the lakes which observe the like periodicity—the organ-grinders, for instance, and "the Poet Close." Every year during the tourist season Close leaves his distant home, and settles himself at Bowness to sell what he calls poetry. He is the son of a Westmoreland butcher, who left his vocation to butcher the Queen's English like a Zulu. On the occasion of the marriage of the late Lord Lonsdale, Close sent him some verses, of which here is a specimen:

"The Honorable William Lowther,
    Our Secretary at Berlin, he,
Respected much at Prussia's court,
    Kept up our dignity.
His nephew, now Lord Lonsdale,
    Upon his wedding day,
We wish all health and happiness,
    All heartily we pray."

Alfred Tennyson never made more money by his finest lyric than Close by the lines I have just quoted. It may be that the Hon. William Lowther, fresh from the country of Goethe, did not read the verses, but only the appeals for help accompanying them; at any rate, he used his influence with Lord Palmerston, who placed the name of "John Close, Poet," on the Pension List. Poor Palmerston never heard the last of it. Sir William Sterling Maxwell, M.P., insisted that the pension should be withdrawn, and so it was, but not until "the Poet Close" had received a hundred pounds in addition to his first pension payments.

"Poet Close" sends his poems to all royal and titled folk in the world, and makes the most of any formal acknowledgment of their receipt which may be returned to him. In response to a remark made·to him on the rare advantage which tourists and residents at Bowness have in seeing a poet selling his works in a book-stall, when so many other poets—the Laureate, for instance—are shy of the public, he answered, grandly, "No man in England, or the wide, wide world, ever did what I have done and am now doing—selling my own books, ay, and corresponding with crowned heads, the late Majesty of France, and England's glorious Queen, and also her future King!" So passeth the glory of Wordsworthshire! There is not now a poet on all that hallowed ground, and straight uprises Close to style himself "the Bard of Westmoreland." The only compensation for this which I found at Bowness was when a really good player on the harp came to our hotel door, accompanied by a young Westmoreland woman who sang sweetly some old Border ballads. Like the Scotch, they are mainly in the sad minor key, as is apt to be the case with songs of a people whose local patriotic memories are hopeless traditions of the past, and survive only in their songs. On the Border even these have become few, but there have been imitations of them, and most of the tunes are somewhat modified Scotch airs.

There was another sign at Bowness of the passing away of ancient glories from the earth. The only interesting building there is a church of respectable antiquity, dedicated to St. Martin, and now the parish church. But from this old church every trace of St. Martin has so utterly passed away that the intelligent young girl who showed us the interior did not seem even to have heard the dear old saint's name. There are fairly preserved remains of a finely stained chancel window (brought from Furness Abbey), in which one may discern the Crucifixion, with the Virgin on one side and St. John on the other, the arms of France and England quartered above, and a group of monks beneath; there are two mitred abbots, and a St. George slaying the dragon. But though around this window and in various parts of the church there are armorial bearings of old families in the

WINDERMERE FERRY.

neighborhood, notably the Flemings, I could find no vestige of the saint who divided his cloak with the beggar, and after whom the first Christian church in England—still standing at Canterbury—was named. The decline of St. Martin before the dragon-slayer is a curious fact. In 1837 the republic of Buenos Ayres came to the conclusion that St. Martin, the patron saint of that country, had not adequately responded to the attentions of the citizens, and they voted his dismission, awarding him, however, as a pension for his ancient services, four wax candles of one pound each and a mass in the cathedral per annum. They elected Ignatius Loyola to the office of patron saint in his place. In England something of the same kind appears to have gradually taken place. Perhaps Martin, being the special weather saint, allowed so much rain-fall that the people gradually gave him up, though whether they got much by it any one who has passed recent years in England may have doubts. The church-yard at Bowness holds the tomb of one good and learned man: it is inscribed "Ricardi Watson, Episcopi Landavensis, cineribus sacrum, obiit Julii 1, A.D. 1816, ætatis 72." This Bishop of Llandaff, author of *The Apology for the Bible*, resided at Calgarth Park,

near by. His father taught school at Haversham, Westmoreland, forty years. The bishop was the most vigorous opponent of Thomas Paine, and in their controversy his learning was graced by a charity little known at that time, and which caused him to remark on the sublimity of Paine's writing concerning the attributes of the Deity.

The rose-window of the dawn was flashing its tints all over Windermere on that July morning when I first gazed upon that beautiful lake. It was like the fairest dream. Green islets made up of trees sat upon it, their foliage perfectly reflected in the translucent surface. Here and there small snowy sails were seen, and the curving wooded shores up and down gave a perfect fringe to the opalescent water. A long range of dark blue hills made a frame for the picture. It was a fascination that drew my friend and me without a word to the edge of the water; and I suspect it was only because we found a boat there, prepared for such fascinations, that my young comrade, an artist, was rescued from the probable result of a mad impulse to swim the lake to Belle Isle. We had soon glided over to it, and were surprised to find no sirens there. But we found them presently, and heard them: a choir of birds, lilies, and oracular oaks, still rehearsing the "prelude" they sang to a boy there a hundred years ago.

"When summer came,
Our pastime was, on bright half-holidays,
To sweep along the plain of Windermere
With rival oars; and the selected bourne
Was now an island musical with birds
That sang and ceased not; now a Sister Isle
Beneath the oaks' umbrageous covert, sown
With lilies-of-the-valley like a field;
And now a third small island, where survived
In solitude the ruins of a shrine
Once to Our Lady dedicate, and served
Daily with chaunted rites."
—WORDSWORTH. *Prelude*, ii.

It appears rather droll at first thought to find that a solid Manchester manufacturer has purchased this island and its pleasant mansion. In ancient times it would have been the home of some saintly hermit—some Godric or Cuthbert—seeking a lonely paradise. One would expect a poet to dwell here. (What an ideal home it would have been for Wordsworth!) But on reflection it is just as pleasant to think of the Manchester man coming all the way up here, and investing so much of his gold in a summer solitude. This is his way of keeping, amid the murky air and moil of Manchester, one window open to the azure. The poets already have their inward Belle Isle, and can better spare this visible one.

At some distance onward, near the southern end of the isle, two swans showed themselves for a moment, then vanished. We rowed that way, but did not see them again. But we presently saw a charming tanglewood and a solitary tower, inhabited by a beautiful maiden and her sharp-eyed female guardian; and, according to all orthodox folk-lore in the world, the swans must have turned into these. That they were Swan-maidens was further suggested by the fact that their tower was close to a ferry, bearing the name of Ferry Nab. The name "Nab" is given to pointed mountainous projections in this neighborhood, as Ben and Pen are used in Scotland and Wales and elsewhere; but in the name of Grimm I repudiate such an explanation of this Nab, which has no more right to be named after a sharp mountain peak than the *nib* of my pen. The mountain nab and the pen nib both come from Anglo-Saxon *nebbe*, a nose. Now anciently, throughout Scotland and all this region, imps, consequently witches, were supposed to

have long noses, and were called "long-nebbed." A venerable friend tells me that he remembers to have heard grace before meat in Scotland in these words: "Frae witches an' warlocks an' a' lang-nebbed creatures, guid Lord deliver us!" I remarked to my comrade that there ought to be some weird legend about this ferry; but our boatman had never heard of any, and of course the Swan-maidens would not confess to any. Nevertheless, in the evening, when we spoke of going over the ferry by moonlight, they told us that under no circumstances did the ferry-boat ever stir after sunset; and on exploring this fact, I found covered up underneath it a tradition that once upon a time a ferryman had responded to a call in the night, and on his return was gloomy, would not say what he had seen, and soon went mad and died. It was a long time ago, and I hope the shade of the poor ferryman will forgive me the satisfaction with which I heard this saga of the Nab, though this is tempered with regret that he left no description of the Nose of the traveller who summoned him at night, and fastened the boat to its moorings for all subsequent nights.

Possibly the phantom by which the ferryman was pursued was the same that pursued young Wordsworth when he was a school-boy in the neighborhood. "It was an act of stealth and troubled pleasure," he tells us, in the "Prelude" (ii.), when one summer evening, finding a boat tied to a willow, he unloosed it, and pushed from shore, fixing his eye upon a craggy summit, *i. e.*, a Nab.

"She was an elfin pinnace; lustily
I dipped my oars into the silent lake,
And, as I rose upon the stroke, my boat
Went heaving through the water like a swan;
When, from behind that craggy steep, till then
The horizon's bound, a huge peak, black and huge,
As if with voluntary power instinct,
Upreared its head. I struck, and struck again,
And growing still in stature, the grim shape
Towered up between me and the stars, and still,
For so it seemed, with purpose of its own,
And measured motion, like a living thing,
Strode after me. With trembling oars I turned,
And through the silent water stole my way
Back to the covert of the willow-tree.
There in her mooring-place I left my bark,
And through the meadows homeward went, in grave
And serious mood; but after I had seen
That spectacle, for many days my brain
Worked with a dim and undetermined sense
Of unknown modes of being; o'er my thoughts
There hung a darkness—call it solitude
Or blank desertion. No familiar shapes

A SWAN-MAIDEN.

Remained, no pleasant images of trees,
Of sea or sky, no colors of green fields;
But huge and mighty forms, that do not live
Like living men, moved slowly through the mind
By day, and were a trouble to my dreams."

Subtract from Wordsworth his power to analyze such an experience as this, his power to detach it from himself and give it body and life in a poem; let the refined scholar relapse into the peasant of the past; and what have you? A superstitious ferryman, with a bad conscience, conjuring a phantom out of yon dark mountain, and losing his wits.

The tower near the ferry is called the "station." It has been built merely as an outlook, and is owned by the proprietor of Belle Isle. The more elderly of the Swan-maidens took us to the upper room of this commonplace edifice, and showed us how the lake and landscape looked through different-colored glasses. The windows, which occupied nearly all of three walls, were of variously colored glass. Looking through one and another of these we were assured we should see the scenery as it appeared in each of the seasons. But my friend the artist was absurdly fastidious; pronounced the autumnal scene a "huckleberry view," and almost dislocated his neck to get at some colorless glass through which he might see the unadorned Windermere. Fortunately the elderly Swan-maiden had no idea of the meaning of huckleberry, and the artist is so suave even in his execrations that we escaped being ourselves transformed. We found the younger Swan-maiden, in the absence of the other, a very merry witch, and were not surprised to learn that she was the rustic belle of the neighborhood—or had been, for she had just plighted her troth to a youth who had won a prize in a walking match.

"Are you not sometimes lonely over here?" we had asked this Swan-maiden.

"Do I look so?" she answered, archly, as she wrung with her white hands a white something from the wash-tub (no doubt part of her plumage).

"Not particularly," we admitted, "but in winter, when it is cold, frozen, snowy, and no tourists pass, and—"

"Ah, we manage to be comfortable even in the winter, and without the tourists."

Then she glanced around the room with a blushing satisfaction, and sure enough it was an abode where happiness might well nestle. Everything was neat and in order, albeit on a washing-day; the tall mahogany clock told true time; the shelves were fairly set with books; and in the cupboard was some blue china which tempted one to covet.

"What do you do on Sundays?"

"Go to church at Satterthwaite."

"Good preacher there?"

For the first time the young Swan-maiden was floated out of her depth.

"Good?" she said, pausing over the tub. "Yes, he's good."

"Oh, I didn't mean that; I meant his preaching—is that good? is he eloquent, interesting, talented?"

It was but too plain that on this young life had never before been pressed the idea of distinguishing between parson and parson. The arrival of the elderly dame from the tower saved her the necessity of entering upon a criticism of the Satterthwaite clergyman. We went off with a pleasant feeling of having interviewed one of those pretty wild flowers of which Wordsworth made so much, and of which there is reason to suspect he sometimes made flowers much more simple and lowly than the originals before they were subjected to his poeticulture.

An example of this may be cited from the "Excursion." One of the sweetest pictures of humble idyllic life in that poem relates to Jonathan and Betty Yewdale, who lived at Little Langdale. Some readers of that passage may suppose that Yewdale is a fancy name, since a beautiful vale near this is so called from its venerable yew-tree, popularly believed to be coeval with the Deluge. But the Yewdales were real people. Wordsworth was lost and benighted in that region, and the only guidance he found was a single light. It seemed to him too high to proceed from a human habitation, yet he climbed toward it and found a cottage. The wife had set the light to guide her husband. He was hospitably welcomed. The husband when he arrived impressed the poet by his manners—"so graceful in his gentleness"—and he thought he must be descended from some illustrious race. Betty's account of their life must be quoted at length:

"'Three dark midwinter months
Pass,' said the matron, 'and I never see,
Save when the Sabbath brings its kind release,
My helpmate's face by light of day. He quits
His door in darkness, nor till dusk returns.
And, through Heaven's blessing, thus we gain the bread
For which we pray, and for the wants provide
Of sickness, accident, and helpless age.
Companions have I many, many friends,
Dependents, comforters—my wheel, my fire,
All day the house-clock ticking in mine ear,
The cackling hen, the tender chicken brood,
And the wild birds that gather round my porch;
This honest sheep-dog's countenance I read,
With him can talk, nor seldom waste a word
On creature less intelligent and shrewd.
And if the blustering wind that drives the clouds
Care not for me, he lingers round my door,
And makes me pastime when our tempers suit;
But above all my thoughts are my support.'"

WINDERMERE, SOUTHWARD VIEW.

Very charming. But some years ago Mr. Gibson, F.S.A., being in the neighborhood, made some inquiries about Jonathan and Betty, and found the latter to be a heroine of a very different kind from what he had gathered from the poet's page. The most vivid reminiscence was given him by an old lady of how Jonathan was brought back home by his wife from a "funeral fray" or festivity at Coniston, where he had remained all night. "Off she set i' t' rooad till Cunniston. On i' t' efterneeun she co' back, driving Jonathan afooer her wi' a lang hezle stick—an' he sartly was a sairy object. His Sūnda' cleeas leeūk't as if he'd been sleepin' i' them on t' top of a durty fluer." Passing over the further graphic description of Jonathan's sorry appearance, crowned with a hat which "hed gitten bulged in at t' side," and also Betty's account of how she had made the funeral meats fly when she found the carousers, I must quote the conclusion of the story. "'Dud iver yè see sike a pictur?' 'Why, nay! nit sa offen, indeed,' says I. 'Well,' says Betty, 'as I wodn't be seen i' t' rooads wi' him, we hed to teeak t' fields for't, an', as it wosn't seeaf ut let him climm t' wo's, I meead him creep t' hog-holes; an' when I gat him in an' his legs out, I did switch him.'"

As we gained the height beyond Bowness, on the road to Ambleside, we paused for some time; and while my comrade the artist—I will call him the Abbé, though he is not in the least sacerdotal—passes an hour of ecstasy over the southward view of Windermere, my eyes were dwelling on an ancient farm and homestead over against the northward water, with which is associated one of the weird legends of this region. Calgarth is the name of it, and it is not picturesque enough for the guide-books to do more than mention it. Miss Martineau praises the owner for leaving depressions in his walls in order that travellers may look across his estate to the scenery beyond, and mentions that the arms of the Phillipsons are still there in the kitchen, carved amid a profusion of arabesque devices over the ample fire-place. But none of our professional guides appear to have got hold of the story of the place as it is known to the more aged peasants. It runs that Calgarth (which seems to be from O. N. *kálgarde*, a vegetable garden) was a bit of ground owned by a humble farmer named Kraster Cook and his good wife Dorothy. But their little inheritance was coveted by the chief aristocrat and magistrate of the neighborhood, Myles Phillipson. The Phillipsons were a great and wealthy family, but they could not induce Kraster and Dorothy to sell them this piece of ground to complete their estate. Myles Phillipson swore he'd have that ground, be they "live or deead;" but as time went on he appeared to be more gracious, and once he gave a great Christmas banquet to the neighbors, to which Kraster and Dorothy were invited. It was a dear feast for them. Phillipson pretended they had stolen a silver cup, and sure enough it was found in Kraster's house— a "plant," of course. The offense was then capital; and as Phillipson was the magistrate, Kraster and Dorothy were sentenced to death. In the court-room Dorothy arose, glowered at the magistrate, and said, with words that rung through the building: "Guard thyself, Myles Phillipson! Thou thinkest thou hast managed grandly; but that tiny lump of land is the dearest a Phillipson has ever bought or stolen; for you will never prosper, neither your breed; whatever scheme you undertake will wither in your hand; the side you take will always lose; the time shall come no Phillipson will own an inch of land; and while Calgarth walls shall stand, we'll haunt it night and day—never will ye be rid of us!" Thenceforth the Phillipsons had for their guests two skulls. They were found at Christmas at the head of a stairway; they were buried in a distant region, but they turned up in the old house again. The two skulls were burned again and again; they were brayed to dust and cast to the wind; they were several years sunk in the lake; but the Phillipsons never could get rid of them. Meanwhile old Dorothy's weird went on to its fulfillment, until the family sank into poverty, and at length disappeared.

The only other famous occupant of Calgarth was the Bishop of Llandaff, already mentioned. This worthy Dr. Watson, who tells us that when he was appointed Professor of Chemistry at Oxford he had never seen any work on that subject, was quite accomplished in the science of ghost-laying. He realized, when he retired to Calgarth for the purpose of learned gardening, that two dead skulls existed in the folk-imagination, and must be laid to rest by the wit of a living skull. So he seems to have done something solemn over an old wall, after which it was agreed that Kraster and Dorothy had consented, in consideration of so good a man, to rest quiet for the future. The present holder of Calgarth is Lieutenant-Colonel Watson, a magistrate, but not of the Phillipson kind, who has gained the good-will of all by his thoughtfulness in keeping open the view through his grounds.

It is strange to find lingering in these northern counties, along with so many Scandinavian and German names and words, the ancient Teutonic idea of the divining power of woman. Tacitus mentions the German custom of consulting the women as oracles. There were times when women alone knew how to read and write, the men being too much engaged with their spears to respect anything done with the pen; but the proverbial miraculousness of the unknown made them ready to regard a mysterious combination of letters as a *spell*. May not many a poor little wife have utilized the tendency to superstition in her huge master by encouraging the notion that a power superior to his lay in her mystic letters? The spae-wife, or spy-wife, seems to have inherited some of the characters of the Parcæ too: her curse could never be reversed.

It is a pity that Sir Walter Scott could not have visited this neighborhood earlier in life than he did. It was only seven years before his death that he made his memorable visit to Christopher North at Elleray, and his knack of getting at good old stories was nearly gone. The Wizard had, however, heard at Abbotsford the chief story of one of these famous Phillipsons, and reproduced it in "Rokeby." Belle Isle, which we have already visited, and which from Elleray appears as a superb emerald on the breast of Windermere, belonged to Colonel Phillipson at the time of the civil war between Charles I. and Parliament. He and his younger brother, a major, were bold champions of the royal cause, and the major went by the name of Robin the Devil. Colonel Briggs, of Cromwell's army, undertook to capture this major, who had taken refuge in his brother's house on Belle Isle. His brother was absent, and the major confirmed his title of "the Devil" by successfully resisting a siege of eight months. His brother having come to his relief, Colonel Briggs was compelled to withdraw from before Belle Isle. But Major Phillipson resolved to avenge the insult, and with a small band of horse went over to Kendal, where Colonel Briggs was stationed. Hearing that the colonel was at church—it was Sunday morning—he posted his men at the church door, and dashed down the aisle on horseback! The colonel was not there. The congregation, at first terror-stricken, made an attempt to arrest the intruder, who galloped down another aisle, but in making his exit struck his head violently against the arch of the doorway. Though his helmet was struck off, and his saddle girth gave way, the stunned warrior struggled with those who tried to capture him, and made his escape. His helmet still hangs in Kendal church. There Sir Walter saw it, and

PROFESSOR WILSON'S COTTAGE AT ELLERAY.

told it of Bertram Risingham, in the sixth canto of "Rokeby."

It may even be that the legend of the Calgarth skulls—for Calgarth then belonged to the Phillipsons—is a mere saga that grew out of the nickname Robin the Devil.

The "Race of Giants," as Christopher North called the mountains seen from his door, and the lakes, needed sorely among their genii one who could preserve their popular traditions. One can hardly forgive Southey for wandering far away into the East to get tales for his poems, when similar ones were growing all around him here. It excites a smile now to find him writing to Coleridge in this way: "I was, and am still, utterly at a loss to devise by what possible means fictions so perfectly like the Arabian tales in character, and yet so indisputably of Cimric growth, should have grown up in Wales." He put some of the Welsh mythology into Madoc, so transferring them to the American aborigines; but he never learned that Dorothy's curse of Calgarth was a better subject for him than the curse of Kehama. As a result of this primitive state of mind among those lords of the Lake, the guide-books are sadly barren of these early romances. The tourist here finds himself much beguided: Wordsworth has written a guide, and Harriet Martineau also. Wordsworth's is, curiously enough, out of print; Harriet Martineau has been so re-done—I will not say edited—that while her reader discovers that, contrary to the general impression, she was a good Christian, he can not give her an equal credential for ready observation of those human characteristics of the neighborhood to which she might have been supposed particularly alive. She does, indeed, mention a haunted house; but unless her invisible re-doer has strangely supplemented her work, she also actually believed in it!

Well, if these worthies did not gather very well the primitive romance of the Lakes, they extemporized a good deal for them which in the course of time will be transformed into a pretty enough mythology. Christopher North was himself a kind of Thor and Baldur in one, with a touch of the frost-giant in him to boot. Now we find him daring dangerous Windermere in a snow-storm, in darkness too, vainly trying for hours to recover shore, and nearly dying of cold. "Master was well-nigh frozen to death," reported his man Billy, "and had icicles a finger long hanging from his hair and beard." Next

17

evening, like as not, he is at Charles Lloyd's fine mansion dancing with the belle of the Lakes—gracefulest dancer he in the district! And when the first breath of spring has called out the wild

JOHN WILSON.

flowers, lo! he is amid them, perhaps calling the Greek Meleager to his aid to tell them how lovely they are, and then how perfect must she be who is lovelier—that aforesaid Belle of Brathay!*

How many diligent readers nowadays know Christopher North? The question "reminds me of a little story." In the last days of the old antislavery agitation, when it was supposed by Boston roughs

* The translation alluded to is so beautiful that I must quote it:

"'Tis now that the white violets steal out the
  spring to greet,
And that among his longed-for showers Narcis-
  sus smiles so sweet.
'Tis now that lilies, upland born, frequent the
  slopes of green,
And that the flowers that lovers love, of all the
  flowers the queen,
Without an equal anywhere, in full-blown beauty
  glows;
Thou know'st it well, Zenophilè — Persuasion's
  flower, the Rose.
Ah! why, ye hills and meadows, does bright
  laughter thus illume
Your leafy haunts? so lavish why, and prodigal
  of bloom?
Not all the wreaths of all the flowers that Spring
  herself might cull
As mine own Virgin e'er could be one-half so
  beautiful!"

and their inspirers that a few abolitionists' heads thrown to the South would dissolve the nascent Confederacy, there was a furious mob in the Music Hall. The uproar was continuous, deafening. The saintly face of Garrison beamed on the crowd, but his voice was unheard; the stately form of Phillips uprose, but not a syllable could be caught even by those on the platform. All efforts at gaining silence having failed, all orators having given up, Wendell Phillips espied in a distant nook the serene face of Emerson. The idea struck him that perhaps that calm face might have some effect. Emerson was persuaded, and advanced to the front. The mob did not know him, and the noise very slightly abated, because some were asking who he was. Emerson began his speech with these words: "Christopher North—of course you all know Christopher North—" These were magic words. Whether it was the compliment to their intelligence, or whether the startling wildness of the proposition that they had ever heard of him, the crowd was instantly hushed, and the mob was chilled and foiled. Emerson went on with a capital speech, and he began it with the story of Christopher North, when rebuked for his anger and violence toward two scamps, declaring that he had treated them with the utmost self-restraint—he had "only pitched them out of the window." Emerson based on that his assertion that the abolitionists had exercised even more self-command under more tempting circumstances; they had been peaceful when it might have been expected they would be revolutionists. But the main force of the speech was in its gentle parenthesis, "Of course you all know Christopher North."

Few indeed are they who know that man, and none who know him only as Professor Wilson, or as a writer. The real man was never got between the arms of a college chair, nor between the covers of a book. He was a character rather than a thinker; a great, handsome, healthy, whole-hearted, generous, heroic soul; a natural noble; one of whom—

reading his life, and the good stories of him, and his works too—we may imagine Krishna as saying to Arjoon, "He my servant is dear unto me who is free from enmity, the friend of all nature; he is my beloved of whom mankind are not afraid, and who of mankind is not afraid." Probably they alone who saw Christopher North amid these lakes and mountains ever really saw him at all. "More than one person," wrote Harriet Martineau, "has said that Wilson reminded them of the first man Adam, so full was his large frame of vitality, force, and sentience. His tread seemed to shake the ground, and his glance to pierce through stone walls; and as for his voice, there was no heart that could stand before it. In his hours of emotion he swept away all hearts whithersoever he would. Not less striking was it to see him in a mood of repose, as he was seen when steering the packet-boat that used to pass between Bowness and Ambleside before the steamers were put upon the lake. Sitting motionless, with his hand upon the tiller, in the presence of journeymen and market-women, his eye apparently looking beyond everything into nothing, and his mouth closed above his beard, as if he meant never to speak again, he was quite as impressive and immortal an image as he could have been to the students of his moral philosophy class, or to the comrades of his jovial hours. He was known, and with reverence and affection, beside the trout stream and the mountain tarn, and amidst the deep gloom of Elleray, where he could not bring himself to let a sprig be lopped that his wife had loved. Every old boatman and young angler, every hoary shepherd and primitive dame, among the hills of the district, knew him and enjoyed his presence. He made others happy by being intensely happy himself, when his brighter moods were on him; and when he was mournful, no one desired to be gay. He has gone with his joy and his grief; and the region is so much darker in a thousand eyes." Miss Martineau became a poet whenever she wrote about the professor, whose health she drank in the first spring breath, and pledged him in the sparkling thunder-shower. "Blessings above all on Christopher North!" she exclaims again; "we can not but wonder whether he ever cast a thought upon such as we are when breasting the breeze on the moors, or pressing up the mount-ain-side, or watching beside the trout stream . . . . Whether he is now conscious of the fact or not, his spirit has come many a time, while his tired body slept, and opened our prison doors, and led us a long flight over mountain and moor, lake and lea, and dropped us again in our beds, refreshed and soothed, to dream, at least, of having felt the long-lost sensation of health once more."

Elleray Cottage, with its "several roofs shelving away there in the lustre of loveliest lichens, each roof with its own assortment of doves and pigeons preening their pinions in the morning pleasaunce," remains, and over it the tutelary sycamore—that sycamore of which Christopher wrote, "Never in this well-wooded world, not even in the days of the Druids, could there have been such another tree; it would be easier to suppose two Shakspeares." Here Wilson passed the eight brightest years of his life; to this spot he brought his bride for the never-waning honey-moon; and though the loss of his little fortune by the dishonesty of an uncle compelled him to leave this cottage (1815), enough was won back when eight years later he was able to take up his summer quarters here again. "He was in a position," writes his daughter, "once more to take up his summer quarters in his beautiful villa of Elleray, the place which he loved above all others on earth; and in the summer of 1823 we find him there, with his wife and children again under the old roof-tree." "He was in the habit of sauntering the whole day long among the woods and walks of Elleray." In one of those fond letters of his to his wife, which hardly bear printing, he says: "The country now is in perfect beauty; and I think of one who has been a kind and affectionate and good wife to me, at all hours. If I do not, may the beauty of nature pass away from my eyes!" It was years after when Jane passed away, and sure enough with her the beauty of Elleray. "Sadly," writes the daughter, "comes the confession from his lips of the dreariness which fell upon him at Elleray, a place at one time as enjoyable as paradise." He tried to go there again, but when he slept at the Bowness hotel "the silence and loneliness of the night to him were not to be borne." He went off, and saw Elleray no more.

Christopher North, in the history of the Lakes, occupies the place of a Prospero;

ROBERT SOUTHEY.

did regattas that ever enlivened Windermere. Perhaps there were not fewer than fifty barges following in the professor's radiant procession when it paused at the point of Storrs to admit into the place of honor the vessel that carried kind and happy Mr. Bolton and his guests. The three bards of the Lakes led the cheers that hailed Scott and Canning; and music and sunshine, flags, streamers, and gay dresses, the merry hum of voices and the rapid splashing of innumerable oars, made up a dazzling mixture of sensations as the flotilla wound its way among the richly foliaged islands, and along bays and promontories peopled with enthusiastic spectators."

"There were giants on the earth in those days." Such was our not very original but sincere remark as we drove on through deep and shady roads toward Troutbeck. "Yes," broke in our driver; "he lived over there," pointing with his whip.

all that this region has known in the way of pageants and revels is associated with his wand. Of these the most notable was that which occurred on the occasion when Sir Walter Scott and Canning came to be the guests of Mr. Bolton, a merchant, at Storrs Hall on Windermere. The host threw his house open to all the literary men —Wordsworth, Wilson, Southey, and the rest—and they staid there night and day. "It would have been difficult," says Lockhart, "to say which star in the constellation shone with the brightest or the softest light. There was 'high discourse,' intermingled with as gay flashings of courtly wit as ever Canning displayed; and a plentiful allowance on all sides of those airy, transient pleasantries in which the fancy of poets, however wise and grave, delights to run riot when they are sure not to be misunderstood. There were beautiful and accomplished women to adorn and enjoy this circle. The weather was as Elysian as the scenery. There were brilliant cavalcades through the woods in the mornings, and delicious boatings on the lake by moonlight; and the last day Professor Wilson ('the Admiral of the Lakes,' as Canning called him) presided over one of the most splen-

"Who?" we asked. "The giant," said the driver, with a look of surprise. He was a taciturn driver, silent as a Trappist; this was his first venture, and, with a view to encourage it, I said, "Oh yes, of course, the giant." We were all expectation, but the driver had no more to say. "Let's see, what was his name, driver?" "Hugh Hird." "He was a tremendous fellow, wasn't he?" "Could lift as much as ten men, and eat a whole sheep." That was all we could get out of our driver concerning the Troutbeck giant. Miss Martineau's account of him is as follows: "Tradition tells of a giant, 'a man of amazing strength,' who lived in Troutbeck Park, in the time of Henry IV. He begged from house to house till he came there, but finding an empty dwelling, he took possession. This house had been forfeited to the crown, and was of so little value that he remained for a time undisturbed. At last a tenant was found, and came to take possession; but the giant, who was 'quite uncivilized, and knew no law but strength,' prevented him. Upon this he was sent to London, where he so pleased the king by his feats of strength that he was promised anything he might ask for. His petition was the house in Troutbeck, the paddock behind it to get peat for fuel, and liberty to cut wood in Troutbeck Park. It is said the king asked him what he lived upon, and his reply was, 'Thick pottage and milk, that a mouse might walk upon dry-shod, for breakfast, and the sunny side of a wedder to his dinner when he could get it' (*i. e.*, the whole of the wether). His mother lived with him, and they toiled on these hill-sides, making a livelihood chiefly by cutting and burning the common brackens, from which they obtained a residue which was used in the manufacture of soap. Their graves are said to be discernible near the old 'hog-house.' This was the estate afterward given by Charles I. to Huddlestone Phillipson for his services in the civil wars."

Although there appears to be no doubt that some man of enormous stature and strength dwelt at Troutbeck, it is not improbable that the tradition has gathered something here and there—a bit from the powerful Phillipson (Robin the Devil), who possessed the place, and a bit from the prehistoric monument at Penrith, called the Giant's Grave. Among other traditions about Hugh Hird, one relates that alone with his bow and arrows he drove back a party of Scotch marauders. It may be remembered, also, that in the time of Henry IV. there was a wide-spread belief in formidable forest phantoms of the *Gros Veneur* order, which were generally called Hugh or Hugo, after the spectre of Hugh Capet in France.

The people in Westmoreland and Cumberland are very fond of athletic exercises, and extraordinary powers are still sometimes developed among them. During the long life of Wordsworth in this region there was one man more famous among the common folk than he, namely, Ben Wells, for fifty years dancing master and fiddler to the country people of Cumberland. Ben was the kind of man who in a more primitive time gave country folk their legends. The instrument being changed, Ben might have been the original of the boy in "A mery Geste of the Frere and the Boye," who had a magic pipe:

> "All that may the pipe here
> Shall not themselfe stere,
> But laugh and lepe about."

He not only made cows and milkmaids dance, but so wrought on a friar that he capered until bit by bit he lost

> "His cope and scapelary,
> And all his other wede."

Mr. Craig Gibson, F.S.A., has written (1869) a lyric about Ben Wells, in the Cumberland dialect, and in a note says: "The last time I met with him was about twenty years ago, in the bar parlor of an inn in the southern part of the Lake district, where the strains of his fiddle, produced

THOMAS DE QUINCEY.

at my request, caused such excitement that a general and very uproarious dance (of males only) set in, and was kept up with such energy that, the space being confined, the furniture was seriously damaged, and Ben was at last ejected by the landlady, as the readiest—indeed, the only —method of putting a stop to the riot. He was light, muscular, and springy, and in his earlier years wonderfully swift of foot, so much so that the late Dr. Johnstone of Cockermouth told me that he once (at Scale Hill) saw him, without any assistance, run down and capture a wild rabbit—a proof of activity rarely paralleled." I quote two verses of Mr. Gibson's poem, which may be read as the

ISAAC WALKER.

reflections of an old Cumbrian on the fiddler's death:

"Ben Wales's fiddle many a neet
   Gev weel-oiled springs to t' heaviest heels,
For few cud whyet hod the'r feet
   When Ben struck up his heartenin' reels.
Wid elbow-room an' rozel't weel,
   Swinge! how he'd mak' fwoke keàv an' prance!
An' nowte cud match t' sly fiddle-squeal
   'At signal'd kiss i' t' cushion-dance.*

"Fwoke's ways turn different, t' langer t' mair,
   An' what, lang sen, was reet's grown wrang;
We're meàst on us ower fine to care
   For heàmly dance, teùn, teàl, or sang.
An' nowte's meàd varra lastin' here;
   T' best bow-hand growes oald an' fails,
An' t' lishest legs git num' an' queer:
   Few last sa weel as oald Ben Wales."

* The cushion-dance is, I believe, peculiar to this district, and is the finishing dance of a rural ball or merry-night. A young man, carrying a cushion, paces round the room in time to the appropriate tune, selects a girl, lays the cushion at her feet, and both kneel upon it and kiss, the fiddler making an extraordinary squeal during the operation. The girl then takes the cushion to another young man, who kisses her as before, and leaves her free to "link" with the first, and march round the room. This is repeated till the whole party is brought in, when they all form a circle, and "kiss out" in the same manner, sometimes varying it by the kissers sitting on two chairs, back to back, in the middle of the ring, and kissing over their shoulders—a trying process (adds Mr. Gibson) to bashful youth of either sex.

Christopher North and De Quincey were fond of "the old Laker" Ritson, who was such a famous wrestler. De Quincey used to take long walks with him, and Christopher North several times contended with him. In their wrestling matches Ritson threw Wilson twice out of three falls, confessing that he found him "a varra bad 'un to lick"; but in running Christopher beat him, and in jumping could manage twelve yards in three leaps, with a heavy stone in each hand, while Ritson could only manage eleven and three-quarters.

The Grasmere sports are still kept up, but the last youth who gained much celebrity at them came to a sad end. Jonathan Park was about twenty-three years of age when he took the first prize for the mountain race at Grasmere—£25, as I heard—but it would seem to have sadly demoralized him. He went upon a long spree, and two days after his prize was won, in August, 1874, he either drowned himself or was drowned in Windermere.

After the Giant comes Jack, too clever for his Hugeness: the small man of skill eats less, accomplishes more; and evolution goes on from the big to the little. The "hog-house" where the giant rests may have given his name to Hogarth, whose ancestors resided in Troutbeck village. The uncle of that great artist resided here, and was famous in the neighborhood for his songs. These were satirical, humorous, and generally about his neighbors. The house of Hogarth's father is still standing in the village, and near it two old trees he is said to have planted. It is a dwelling not mean, but uniquely commonplace there; for the houses of Troutbeck are rather striking, having many gables, and pretty porticoes made of slate-stone. The house where the Hogarths would have lived, if such things were arranged with reference to the fitness of things as seen by later generations, is that of Mr. George Browne, whose wife, in his absence, most kindly and intelligently told us the history of the quaint old furniture with which the house is filled. This charming cottage, with its chimneys transformed into ivy towers, and its walls set with Queen Anne windows framed in climbing-roses and morning-glories, would drive a London pre-Raphaelist "mad with sweet desire." But Mr. Browne is also an amateur worker in wood, and his imitations of ancient cabinets and chests are such as might easily deceive one not familiar with old furniture. This, however, is not his business, and the visitor's hungry eye must train itself to love these art-flowers, and leave them on their stem.

A little beyond this we went to seek out an ancient inn, which bore the name of "The Mortal Man," and which was said to have a curious old sign, representing two men, one fat and jolly, the other haggard, with an appropriate quatrain beneath. When we reached the little inn, however, it was only to discover that the sign had long ago disappeared. We found a better treasure in mine host of "The Mortal Man," as solid, sensible, and honest a specimen of a Westmoreland yeoman as one could imagine. Isaac Walker (such was his name) knew well what would be the value of the sign if he could get it, and he had preserved with the utmost care every antique thing about the house, such as an oak cupboard (three hundred years old at least) in the wall, and some letters on the outside wall, with date, "I. C., 1689." The initials are those of Isaac Cookson, and Isaac Walker's mother was a Cookson. He also repeated to us the correct version of the lines which were on the sign from which the inn derived its name:

"Thou Mortal Man, that lives on bread,
  What is't that makes thy nose so red?—
  Thou silly ass, that looks so pale,
  It is by drinking Sally Birkett's ale."

Having enjoyed the fresh eggs, home-made bread, glasses of cream, pure butter, which excellent Mrs. Walker prepared for us, we sat down together outside the door, and while the Abbé was quietly abducting Isaac's portrait, I listened to his delightful talk about the neighborhood. "It's an old Troutbeck riddle for strangers that, small as the village seems, it has three hundred bulls, constables, and bridges. The township was divided into three parts, called 'hundreds,' and each had a constable, a bull, and a bridge. But old things go. We haven't any ghosts nowadays—Troutbeck railway station's too near. I can remember when a boy would run fit to break his neck past an old lime-kiln near this, because of a ghost—somebody murdered there by being thrown into the kiln. But there are very few superstitions among us now; and the fewer the better." Just here Mrs. Walker came holding triumphantly in her hand the largest egg that hen ever laid—a double egg, which weighed nearly a pound. "It's Becky's egg," said she, whereupon Isaac laughed till his sides shook. "You see," he explained, "there

KITCHEN OF "THE MORTAL MAN."

was a deal ado about that chicken. The old hen got killed—or something happened—and my wife took that half-hatched egg, and carried it about in her bosom, and slept with it, and got to love it before it was born. She says, 'If it's a cock, it's name shall be Jacob, and if it's a hen, it shall be Rebekah.' And so Rebekah it is, and she's paid for all that pains by laying fine eggs, until now she's laid this big one."

Wordsworth, thou shouldst have lived to see this hour! So I mentally exclaimed, then said to Isaac Walker, "The poet Wordsworth would have made a poem about your wife carrying about that egg so tenderly."

"Ah!" said he, without the least anticipation of the effect his words would have on me, "I dare say he would; he was a great man for taking notice of little things."

"Then you have read Wordsworth's poems?" I inquired.

"Not so much that, but when I was a lad I lived with him."

"Lived with him!"

"Ay, for some time, and it is a very well remembered time for me. I was put out to service in a family at Ambleside, and when my master and mistress wanted to travel away in foreign countries, they asked Mr. Wordsworth to take me, just to keep me out of mischief. So I staid in his service at Rydal about a year."

I need not give the questions that now fell thick and fast on old Isaac Walker. The examination had the following results: "Mr. Wordsworth was a plain-looking man, with thin face and large features, especially a pretty big nose. He lived very plainly. He had not a bit of pride, and would talk familiarly but gravely with servants. He used to talk with me kind-ly and familiarly, and I had a warm affection for him. He liked to be out-of-doors whenever he could. Sometimes he was picking up things to look at them, and then he was talking to things in a very queer way. I can see him now, following a bumble-bee all over the garden; he puts his hands behind him this way, and then bends over toward the bee, and wherever it went he followed, making a noise like it — 'Boom-oom-oom-oom.'" Isaac imitated the action and the sound perfectly, but said he could never get the bee's sound so well as Mr. Wordsworth had it. "He would stick to that bee long and long, until it went away; you might go away and come back, and still you would see him striding after that bee, with his mouth down toward it, and hear his 'Boom-oom-oom.' But there was nothing he didn't take notice of. I don't remember so well his friends who used to come and see him; the one I remember most was Mr. Hartley Coleridge, who was a little fellow—carried his head on one side. I remember well Professor Wilson; he was a splendid man, very active and strong. 'The Mortal Man' was his favorite inn over here; but that was before my

LAKE-SIDE.

FELICIA HEMANS.

time. I was sorry to leave Rydal Mount when the time came."

Proud to have been the first that ever burst into this little tarn of Wordsworthian reminiscence in Troutbeck Valley, we set out for Ambleside. The road along which we move so merrily, listening to the voice of bird or water-fall, is in that valley wherein the Britons took refuge from the Romans when these were building their great road from Kendal to Penrith along the ridge of Troutbeck Hills. Where those conquerors left serfs in their Saxon huts there is now a remarkably happy community; and all the wars of Cæsar have hardly so large a place in their traditions as a certain famous contest between a Troutbeck bull and an Orrest Head bull. Josiah Brown of the latter place had a tremendous bull, and some man at Troutbeck had another; and there was so much brag on each side that it was agreed to have a fight between the animals. The terms were that the winner should have the fallen animal, and that they were to meet half way between the two places. It was a tremendous battle. The whole country for many miles around gathered, and Josiah came riding on the back of his monster. The Troutbeck bull was prodigious, and fought furiously; the struggle was like hills hurled against each other, and shook the earth. Finally, the Troutbeck animal fell, and Josiah Brown, having presented it to the poor of Troutbeck, rode back on his victorious bull to Orrest Head. It is safe to say that Rome in her palmiest days never had such a combat as that.

I must own to an emotion of deep delight at the first sight of Dovenest. It was not because, as it nestled amid the trees on a gentle slope of the hill, it seemed the very cottage of which Moore sang,

"I said if there's peace to be found in the world,
   The heart that is humble might hope for it here;"

but it was because sometime Dovenest gave shelter and repose to Felicia Hemans, at a time when hard events seemed to be rechristening her Infelicia. I know that it has long been out of fashion to admire Mrs. Hemans, or even to read her poems; and one must admit that it is before a higher literary canon that her writings have declined in value. But there are regions of experience where literary taste blends with memories of past emotion. No criticism can demonstrate out of existence the facts of human nature. I have heard a learned symphony that left me critical, approving, cold; then heard a child singing with reedy voice some little song familiar in early days, which quickened the pulse and started tears to the eyes: green fields were in it, and the sweet playmates, and the long-lost realm of childhood's sunshine. What can art do better than to raise the happiest emotions? What can I read on the page of Goethe, of Wordsworth, or Tennyson, which can set all these birds and flowers and laden bees around Dovenest singing the songs that evoke from the shadowy past sweet loving faces of those who sang them to me in life's rosy morning-time?

"But what awak'st thou in the heart, O spring—
   The human heart, with all its dreams and sighs—
Thou that giv'st back so many a buried thing;
   Restorer of forgotten harmonies?
Fresh songs and scents break forth where'er thou art—
         What wak'st thou in the heart?

"Too much, oh, there too much! We know not well
   Wherefore it should be thus; but, roused by thee,
What fond strange yearnings from the soul's deep cell
Gush for the faces we no more shall see!
How are we haunted in the wind's low tone
         By voices that are gone!

"Looks of familiar love that never more,
   Never on earth, our aching eyes shall greet,
Past words of welcome to our household door,
   And vanished smiles and sounds of parted feet:
Spring, 'mid the murmurs of thy flowering trees,
         Why, why reviv'st thou these?"

So sang she; and now she is blended with the spring-tide breath which has called up around Dovenest the "fairy-peopled world of flowers," which here made for her the fairest days of her life.

It was just such a beautiful summer evening as this, fifty years ago, as we write these words, that the lovely lady, still a girl after thirty-six summers (more brief, alas! than the winters), stepped into the door at Rydal Mount, and received her cordial greeting from the great poet whose power she was among the first to recognize. "My nervous fear at the idea of presenting myself alone to Mr. Wordsworth grew upon me so rapidly that it was more than seven before I took courage to leave the inn. I had, indeed, little cause for such trepidation. I was driven to a lovely cottage-like building, almost hidden by a profusion of roses and ivy; and a most benignant old man greeted me in the porch; this was Mr. Wordsworth himself; and when I tell you that, having rather a large party of visitors in the house, he led me to a room apart from them, and brought in his family by degrees, I am sure that little trait will give you an idea of the considerate kindness which you will both like and appreciate. In half an hour I felt myself as much at ease with him as I had been with Sir Walter in half a day. I laughed to find myself saying, on the occasion of some little domestic occurrence, 'Mr. Wordsworth, how could you be so giddy?' He has undeniably a lurking love of mischief, and would not, I think, be half so safely trusted with the tied-up bag of winds as Mr. —— insisted that Dr. Channing might be. There is an almost patriarchal simplicity, an absence of all pretension, about him, which I know you would like; all is free, unstudied—'the river winding at its own sweet will'; in his manner and conversation there is more of impulse about them than I had expected, but in other respects I see much that I should have looked for in the poet of meditative life; frequently his head droops, his eyes half close, and he seems buried in quiet depths of thought. I have passed a delightful morning to-day in walking with him about his own richly shaded grounds, and hearing him speak of the old English writers, particularly Spenser, whom he loves, as he himself expresses it, for his 'earnestness and devotedness.'" A few days later she is established as a guest at Wordsworth's house, and finds that the poet's "gentle and affectionate playfulness in the intercourse with all the members of his family would of itself sufficiently refute Moore's theory in the *Life*

RYDAL MOUNT.

of Byron with regard to the unfitness of genius for domestic happiness." It was to her that Wordsworth warmly repudiated the said theory. "It is not," he said, "because they possess genius that they make unhappy homes, but because they do not possess genius enough: a higher order of mind would enable them to see and feel all the beauty of domestic ties." Poor lady! she was then parted from her husband forever, but assuredly not through *her* inability to make and enjoy a beautiful home.

Some of the glimpses which Mrs. Hemans has enabled us to take into Rydal Mount in those days are charming enough. "Imagine, my dear, a bridal present made by Mr. Wordsworth to a young lady in whom he is much interested—a poet's daughter too! You will be thinking of a brooch in the shape of a lyre, or a butterfly-shaped aigrette, or a forget-me-not ring, or some such small gear: nothing of the sort, but a good, handsome, substantial, useful-looking pair of scales to hang up in her store-room! 'For you must be aware, my dear Mrs. Hemans,' said he to me, very gravely, 'how necessary it is occasionally for every lady to see things weighed herself.' *Poveretta me!* I looked as good as I could, and happily for me the poetic eyes are not very clear-sighted, so that I believe no suspicion derogatory to my notability of character has yet flashed upon the master's mind; indeed, I told him that I looked upon the scales as particularly graceful things, and had great thoughts of having my picture taken with a pair in my hand." She tried to get Wordsworth to like Goethe; but he said "Goethe's writings can not live, because they are not holy." "I found that he had unfortunately adopted this opinion from an attempt to read *Wilhelm Meister*, which had inspired him with irrepressible disgust. However, I shall try to bring him into a better way of thinking, if only out of my own deep love for what has been to me a source of intellectual joy, so cheering and elevated."*

---

* The attempt was unsuccessful. Three years later Emerson found Wordsworth still abusing *Wilhelm Meister*. "He had never gone farther than the first part; so disgusted was he that he threw the book across the room." Emerson pleaded for the better parts of the book, "and he courteously promised to look at it again."

WORDSWORTH'S WALK, RYDAL MOUNT.

II.

THE glowing sunset has changed Windermere into a vast opal. On the hills we are leaving the cattle are standing still, as if carved in relief against the sky—a sign of fair weather to-morrow, the driver says. We pass an ancient grove, to which innumerable rooks are noisily repairing for their rest. The driver says he never heard of the notion we had suggested, that they bring good luck to a house, but knew that they pecked out lambs' eyes, and that they make good pie to eat! And we pass the "unpretending rill," which a happy day with his sister beside it made more sacred to Wordsworth "than Ganges or the Nile"; and so, after a glorious little journey, we drive on into Ambleside. The town is rather merry, for it is the second rush-bearing day. Ambleside is one of the two or three towns in the country where this ancient ceremony is observed. The observance is supposed to date from the time of Gregory IV., who recommend-

EAGLE CRAG.

" When from behind that craggy steep, till then
The horizon's bound, a huge peak, black and huge,
As if with voluntary power extinct,
Upreared its head."—WORDSWORTH'S " PRELUDE."

with the prestige of the old. Instead of the rushes which used to be strewn on the floor of the church, garlands of flowers are now borne by a procession of village girls on the last Sunday in July, and they are removed on Monday, when a sermon is preached. Entering Ambleside, I observed two "Druidic" stones set up before a shop for gate posts.

A moonlight row on Windermere, who can tell its charms? Far out on the soft, motionless water, watching the lights on shore, each making its comet tail in the still lake, gliding at our own sweet will, and across the reflex of many a star; pausing now and then to count the sounds faintly wafted through the slumberous air—a dog's bark turned to music by aural perspective, a lonely night bird, or call of the water-fowl; looking up to the sky, radiant with stars double as large and clear as any visible in London—so passed we our first evening by Ambleside. Voyaging round a promontory dense with green foliage, which made a dark path in the water, we neared the mouth by which the Rothay and the Brathay bring their united waters into the lake. The Rothay comes from singing its gentle praises beside the hallowed graves of Grasmere; the Brathay comes with its sobbing dirge for the beauty and the joy that briefly lit up its banks, then withered amid pain, and made it a name of desolation.

For Brathay is associated with Charles Lloyd, a man much valued by the Lake poets, and who combined with Charles Lamb and Coleridge to give the world a volume of poems in 1797. The triad was lampooned in the *Anti-Jacobin Review* as "the anarchists," and Gilray caricatured Coleridge with ass's ears, Lamb as a frog, and Lloyd as a toad. Lloyd trans-

ed the early missionaries in England to rededicate the pagan temples and observe their festivals, so as to invest the new faith lated "Alfieri," and Coleridge wrote that in his babyhood Genius had plunged him "in the wizard fount hight Castaly." Yet Charles Lloyd would appear to have been quite forgotten. He was not indeed a great poet, but he was a fine scholar, a graceful writer, and his mansion, called Low Brathay, his brilliant hospitalities, the joy and tragedy of his life, form much of the romance of this region. Painful histories Wordsworth. Lloyd said to De Quincey: "Ay, that landscape below, with its quiet cottage, looks lovely, I dare say, to you; as for me, I see it, but I feel it not at all." Coleridge, in his "Ode to Dejection," looking during a serene eve on clouds, stars, and crescent, exclaims:

"I see them all so excellently fair,
I see, not feel, how beautiful they are."

Wordsworth, on the other hand, elevated

RYDAL WATER.

have strangely haunted this picturesque country, but few so sorrowful as that of Lloyd. The son of a wealthy banker, who allowed him plenty of money for himself and his literary friends, he came here to reside with his wife (whom he had married while at Cambridge University), and began to write poems expressive of his happiness and his beautiful home on the Brathay. Insanity having been hereditary in the family, this young man appears to have surrendered to its first faint premonitions in his own case as the summons of fate. He then plucked up courage to struggle; he took exercise and anodynes. An ingenious writer, the author of *Business*, in an unpublished volume which I have seen, remarks that the processes of Charles Lloyd's disturbed mind correspond with descriptions written by Coleridge and by the gorgeous vision described in the second book of "The Excursion," speaks of Blea Tarn—

"This little vale, a dwelling-place of man,
Lay low beneath my feet; 'twas visible—
I saw not, but I felt that it was there."

Again, Lloyd told De Quincey that he seemed to hear a "dull trampling sound .... the sound of some man, or party of men, continually advancing slowly, continually threatening, or continually accusing him .... again and again .... he caught the sullen and accursed sound, trampling and voices of men, or whatever it were, still steadily advancing." Coleridge says, in "The Pains of Sleep":

"But yesternight I prayed aloud
In anguish and in agony,
Upstarting from the fiendish crowd
Of shapes and thoughts that tortured me;

31

THE KNOLL.

intervals from France to England upon business connected with the interests of her family; and during one of these visits she came to the Lakes, where she selected Grasmere for her residence, so that I had opportunities of seeing her every day for the space of several weeks. Otherwise I never saw any of the family except one son, an interesting young man, who sought most meritoriously, by bursting asunder the heavy yoke of constitutional inactivity, to extract a balm for his own besetting melancholy from a constant series of exertions in which he had forced himself to engage for promoting education or religious knowledge among his poorer neighbors. But often and often, in years after all was gone, I have passed old Brathay, or have gone over purposely after dark, about the time when for many a year I used to go over to spend the evening; and, seating myself on a stone by the side of the mountain river Brathay, have staid for hours listening to the same sound to which so often Charles and I used to hearken together with profound emotion and awe—the sound of pealing anthems, as if streaming from the open portals of some illimitable cathedral; for such a sound does actually arise, in many states of the weather, from the peculiar action of the river Brathay upon its rocky bed; and many times I have heard it of a quiet night, when no stranger could have been persuaded to believe it other than the sound of choral chanting—distant, solemn, saintly. Its meaning and expression were, in these earlier years, uncertain and general; not more pointed or determinate in the direction which it impressed upon one's feeling than the light of setting suns, and sweeping, in fact, the whole harp of pensive sensibilities rather than striking the chord of any one specific sentiment. But since the ruin or dispersion of that household, after the smoke had ceased to ascend from their hearth, or the garden walks to re-echo their voices, oftentimes, when lying by

A lurid light, a trampling throng,
Sense of intolerable wrong,
And whom I scorned those only strong."

Lloyd was overmastered. The owner of Low Brathay—mansion of brilliant hospitality, amidst whose festivities De Quincey first saw Professor Wilson, dancing with his future wife, then the leading belle of the Lake country—was torn from all its joys and treasures of heart and intellect, and lodged in an asylum. De Quincey has told of Lloyd's escape after some years of confinement, and his sudden entry into Grasmere. The wanderer refused the shelter of De Quincey's home; he set out in the evening for his old home. When the two reached Rydal Mere, Lloyd stopped and poured out his sorrows for an hour by the side of the gloomy water; the friends then separated. Lloyd fled into the darkness. After being several times put in an asylum, after temporary liberation or escape, he was sent to a house in France for treatment, and there died.

"I am dearly fond of Charles Lloyd," wrote Charles Lamb; "he is all goodness, and I have too much of the world in my composition to feel myself thoroughly deserving of his friendship."

Charles Lloyd ought to be famous, if only because his memory inspired a passage concerning him by De Quincey hardly surpassed by any prose writing in the English language for solemn eloquence: "Charles Lloyd never returned to Brathay after he had once been removed from it, and the removal of his family soon followed. Mrs. Lloyd, indeed, returned at the river-side, I have listened to the same aerial, saintly sound, whilst looking back to that night, long hidden in the forest of receding years, when Charles and Sophia Lloyd, now lying in foreign graves, first dawned upon me, coming suddenly out of rain and darkness; then young, rich, happy, full of hope, belted with young children (of whom also most are long dead), and standing apparently on the verge of a labyrinth of golden hours. Musing on the night in November, 1807, and then upon the wreck that had been wrought by a space of fifteen years, I would say to myself sometimes, and seem to hear it in the songs of this watery cathedral, 'Put not your trust in any fabric of happiness that has its root in man or the children of men.' Sometimes, even, I was tempted to discover in the same music a sound such as this: 'Love nothing, love nobody, for thereby comes a killing curse

ain river, a more solemn, if a less agitated, admonition—a requiem over departed happiness, and a protestation against the thought that so many excellent creatures, but a little lower than the angels, whom I have seen only to love in this life—so many of the good, the brave, the beautiful, the wise—can have appeared for no higher purpose or prospect than simply to point a moral, to cause a little joy and many tears, a few perishing moons of happiness and years of vain regret. No! that the destiny of man is more commensurate with the grandeur of his endowments, and that our own mysterious tendencies are written hieroglyphically in the vicissitudes of day and night, of winter and summer, and throughout the great alphabet of nature."

But the night has deepened on Windermere. The moon is low, and the lake has drawn over it a sheet of white mist;

STICKLE TARN.

in the rear.' But sometimes, also, very early on a summer morning, when the dawn was barely beginning to break, all things locked in sleep, and only some uneasy murmur or cockcrow in the faint distance, giving a hint of resurrection for earth and her generations, I have heard, in that same chanting of the little mount-

the stars have veiled themselves, and warn us to the shore. There, sure enough, we find them all radiant again, and beneath them a merry score or two of villagers dancing to music of a violin, which shows that "oald Ben Wales" is still marching on. My reverie ends with a happy reminder that mirth and joy will still bloom on where pain and death have passed, and that whatever be the agonies, our little life, like this full day, is rounded with a sleep.

As we pass out of Ambleside we pause to observe a group of children stationary around some absorbing scene. A nearer approach reveals at the centre of this admiring circle an artist with his easel set out on a small grassy triangle between converging streets. Indefatigable artist, sketching, no doubt, the long sweep of Windermere, and the crags of Coniston! But no; our artist's eyes are bent earthward: six yards before him, prostrate on the grass, with small bundle near him, is an ancient wayfarer, who has there apparently passed the night, and has not yet awakened to his fame. His long hair is dishevelled on his shoulders; his long tangled beard falls on his breast; his knee-breeches fall short of his gray stockings by several inches, leaving his knees bare and blue with the cold of the night; his coat is antediluvian with its quaint cut and brass buttons; his coarse striped shirt lies open about his neck and breast. He is indeed a picture. Such figures still haunt these weird ravines and hills, and they used to be characteristic. They are "survivals;" ancient folk of Westmoreland and Cumberland who have fallen on new and strange scenes and times, and can not keep abreast with civilization. "Hermits," as such were called, have nearly disappeared now before the presence of irreverent tourists; but Ambleside still cherishes the memory of one who bore the reputation of a saint until he was taken to a lunatic asylum, where he died not long ago. He dwelt in a hut somewhere amid the hills near Ullswater, and was long regarded with some awe as a man of preternatural knowledge. He loved these hills and vales in his own way as devotedly as Wordsworth himself. Who knows but he was a mute, inglorious Wordsworth, a poet in the rough, whom the mere fact of his never having seen the inside of a college consigned to an asylum instead of Parnassus?

A little way from where the artist and his slumbering model are surrounded by their village admirers is "The Knoll," a charming villa completely covered with ivy, the garden gay with flowers, where Harriet Martineau passed so many happy years. Adjacent is a pleasant Wesleyan chapel, and many a time, while she and Mr. Atkinson and their friends were conversing on philosophy, the hymns and prayers of these humble worshippers must have floated in through the windows, and mingled with the fragrance of the roses climbing over them. Harriet never wrote a word against or about this chapel, which almost touches "The Knoll." The only thing that troubled her was the ugly church steeple, which obtruded itself upon her every outlook, and one can hardly help sympathizing with her offended taste. The biography of Harriet Martineau is too fresh in the mind of the reading world for me to write much about her here. I was pleased to find that, notwithstanding her heresies, the common people in Ambleside held her in gentle and kindly remembrance. She was a good neighbor, charitable to all, considerate toward the unlettered, never cynical or ill-tempered, always cheerful and happy as the roses and ivy of "The Knoll" she so much loved. No one ever pondered more profoundly and lovingly the mystery of nature than she, and she often saw much in scenes least regarded by ordinary eyes. For instance, she admired the small tarns, which are so apt to be eclipsed by the great lakes, and rejoiced in the good work they are doing.

"After rain, if the waters came down all at once, the vales would be flooded—as we see, very inconveniently, by the consequences of improved agricultural drainage. The tarns are a security, as far as they go, and at present the only one. The lower brooks swell after the rain, and pour themselves into the rivers, while the mountain brooks are busy in the same way, emptying themselves into the tarns. By the time the streams in the valley are subsiding the upper tarns are full, and begin to overflow; and now the overflow can be received in the valley without injury." Her sympathy with human excellence never fails because of her general dissent from the beliefs with which it may be associated. Whether it be the charity of tarns or of faithful ministers, she recognizes its greatness. Writing of little Newfield church, where the Rev. Robert Walker served so nobly a poor population for sixty long years, Miss Martineau wrote: "The church is little loftier or larger than the houses near. If it were not for the bell, the traveller would hardly distinguish it as a church on approaching; but when he has reached it he will see the porch, and the little grave-yard with a few tombs, and the spreading yew, encircled by a seat of stones and turf, on which the early comers sit and rest till the bell calls them in. A little dial on a whitened post in the middle of the inclosure tells the time to the neighbors who have no clocks. Just outside the wall is a white cottage, so humble that the stranger thinks it can not be a parsonage, though the climbing roses and glittering evergreens, and clear lattices and pure uncracked walls, make it look as if it might be. He walks slowly past the porch, and sees some one who tells him that it is indeed Robert Walker's dwelling, and who courteously invites him to see the scene of those life-long charities. Here it was that the distant parishioners were fed on Sundays with broth, for which the whole week's supply of meat was freely bestowed. Hither it was that in winter he sent the benumbed children in companies from the school in the church to warm themselves at the single household fire, while he himself sat by the altar during the whole of the school hours, keeping warmth in him by the exercise of the spinning-wheel."

LANGDALE PIKES.

Standing in front of "The Knoll," where the old lady used to sit in the sunshine, as she passed down the gentle flower-wreathed path that led from a life of toil to a peaceful grave, fair Nature appeared to me a more bountiful mother than her children have yet recognized. Here on her great breast she has nourished and soothed with impartial love the pious Felicia and the heretical Harriet, devout Wordsworth and skeptical Shelley, men of the world seeking respite from commercial cares, and mystics moving in worlds unrealized.

When days are clear in the Lake district they are wondrously clear. As we drive on this radiant morning toward Coniston the very seams of the rocks on distant mountains are seen, the snowy torrents are visible even to the beads of their foam, and we can see their furze so plainly that we almost listen to hear the droning of the bees amid it. When we arrived at those tarns about which Miss Martineau wrote so earnestly, and stopped for the Abbé to sketch the chief of them and the hills rising beyond, I watched the surface of these liquid mirrors, and they sometimes were strange as magic mirrors. Once in particular the wind swept rather strongly over the large one near us, and it seemed to darken with reflections of frowning faces in the air— vague indefinable shapes not in the clear sky nor on the hills. The wind drew its own weird pictures on the water. I had never before seen such an effect. A little later and the same wind which had suddenly sprung up summoned from an unseen cloud-land a number of clouds of various shades, which all seemed swiftly sailing southward, as if definitely guided to some common point. There must have lected fairy-land for the purpose. Some of these young people are readers of Wordsworth too. At least I judge so from having heard one of these youths, who came in hungry, call for trout with the re-

HONEY-MOONING.

been a congress of aerial genii somewhere that afternoon. How they frescoed the hills and vales with their shadows! The great Langdale Pikes even seemed to nod in the distance. The vast landscape seemed astir; the mighty hills once more melted and waved under the ebb and flow of cloud-shadows. In no two looks could one see the same landscape, or the same mountain or lake, so often were they transformed by this revolutionary movement of light clouds.

Arrived at the fine hotel at Coniston Water—the Waterhead Hotel—we found ourselves in land where the honey-moon blooms with notable resplendence. It was beaming on two young faces in the dining-room (though slightly clouded so long as *our* luncheon lasted), and out on the lawn, wherever we ventured to seek a good point of view, we had the misfortune to startle young people rehearsing their honey-moonlight sonatas. We could not but acknowledge that Coniston was a well-se-

mark to his bride, "To me the humblest trout that swims could give thoughts too deep for tears!" The bride, being poetical, was properly shocked. It is generally young university men whom one meets in this neighborhood. One never meets with any roughs (always excepting holidays), rarely with any vulgar people. It has been of old the favorite place for reading parties of university under-graduates to come and enjoy walking, boating, bathing, talking, while they are completing their studies for examination. They are genial, affable, hearty, and there is no other place where Young England may be seen to such advantage.

Mr. John Ruskin's villa, Brantwood, is visible just across the head of Coniston Water. Since his severe illness, and his leaving the State Professorship of Art at Oxford, which sorely taxed a man so conscientious in the fulfillment of his duties, Mr. Ruskin has much improved in health. And if Manchester would only turn Thirlmere Lake into its reservoir, or else abandon the notion, this brilliant author might be expected to live long and peacefully in his charming abode. But he is now haunted by the phantasm of moiling Manchester swallowing up his favorite lake, as the giant Thor tried to swallow up the sea. The god of the Hammer failed then, and the city of the Hammer may fail now. But one might think so benevolent a gentleman might find something picturesque in Thirlmere going to refresh and wash the million toilers in the mills. The founder of the new Society of St. George might now be represented as an armed saint contending with a dragon (whose horns will be factory chimneys), to prevent its devouring a fair Lady of the Lake. But why should he not be equally chivalrous for the Manchester ladies actually in the dragon's mouth? It has occurred to me, when listening to this unique man, whose talk is equally charming in public and private, to speculate what might have been the result had he possessed a little more humor. His satire sometimes almost amounts to it, but never quite reaches it. Had he the power of Carlyle to laugh heartily, he would have been a happier man; but would the world have had its great art-critic? Laughter and humor depend on incon-

gruities, and anything incongruous, grotesque, out of proportion, gives Ruskin as much pain as a cut from a knife.

Mr. Ruskin appears to me to have been for some time a living illustration of the development of the artistic nature which Goethe has mystically dramatized in the second part of *Faust*. As Faust finds in Art (symbolized by Helena) merely the raiment of the real Art, the art of Life, and floats away on her garment to be set before his task, in accomplishing which he finds repose, so has this fine artist of England become impatient of mere pictorial beauty, and to demand fiercely the reality it seemed to promise him. He has sold most of his beautiful pictures, and come to sit down in full view of Coniston Old Man—a great, rugged mountain (it is 2633 feet), a perfect symbol of wild strength in repose. Here he is scheming and planning that ideal village community on which he can look, and then lie down amid the roses, and say, with dying Faust, "Remain—thou art fair."

He has some cultured and sympathetic neighbors, among these Mr. and Mrs. Marshall, of Monk Coniston—a mansion possessing pleasant and picturesque grounds. We were indebted to Mrs. Marshall for advice as to our further wanderings which we found very useful. As for the man-

THIRLMERE.

SCHOOL-HOUSE, HAWKESHEAD.

sion, although something has been done to improve the original structure, the Abbé found the ancient farm-house occupied by one of their tenants more to his purpose.

The next point made for was Hawkeshead. This village presents more of the signs of antiquity than any other in the Lakes; there are probably few in England that can show such quaint old houses, with so much well-carved wood-work about them. Here is an ancient Baptist chapel, and I can well believe in the justice of its reputation as among the oldest of the Dissenting places of worship in this kingdom. There is also an old meeting-house of the Quakers, standing apart, snow-white, in its peaceful grove. Yet these buildings are mere things of yesterday compared with a farm-house near the road, whose mullioned window arrested our attention. In this house several of the monks of Furness Abbey resided, and the abbots held their manor courts in the room lighted by that mullioned window. It was in this ancient town that Wordsworth was sent to school, and by far the best of his poetry is connected with it, and the development of his mind in boyhood under the influence of nature.

We carried some introduction to the master of the famous school, Mr. H. T. Baines, whom we found thoroughly informed about all we desired to know in that neighborhood. The ancient school-room is kept so clean and ventilated that one could not imagine its great age were it not for the desks and benches. These have been so notched, dated, autographed, by many generations of boys, that an urchin now could hardly find space for the smallest initial. Perhaps the care with which the masters have for a long time guarded with pride the signatures of the brothers Wordsworth may have given rise to a notion among the lads that to cut one's name there is the first step toward becoming a poet or a bishop. There can have been few Hawkeshead boys, judging by the wood-cuts they have left, who have not shown something of the Wordsworthian aspiration to make a name in the world, and date it.

RUBBING OF WORDSWORTH'S NAME.

Mr. Baines takes great care of the archives of his school. In one of the upper rooms there is a library of old and well-bound books. The school was founded by Edwyne Sandys, Archbishop of York, in 1585. The large and elaborate charter issued by Queen Elizabeth is still perfect. The parchment is decorated with a contemporary full-length portrait of Elizabeth on her throne, and with the symbols of her kingdom, as described in her title—"Elizabeth Regina, Anglie, Francie, et Hiberne." The lion and unicorn, harp and shamrock, are there, but instead of the Scotch thistle there is the French lily. All these illuminations, including the portrait, were made by the hand. The ancient "Rules" of the school are in Archbishop Sandys's handwriting; they prescribe, among other queer things, that the master must not enter public-houses on the days of fairs, nor participate in cock-fights, nor wear a dagger. Hawkeshead was a market-town, with four fairs a year, and such regulations were very important. The archbishop's Bible, metal-bound (1572), containing his family register, is also kept here. Among the sponsors for his grandchildren I observed the name of Washington recurring: Sir John Washington, 1621; Lady Washington, 1629; Mrs. Margaret Washington, 1632 and 1636. It was pleasant to see this name associated with that of the brave chancellor who preferred going to the Tower rather than proclaim Mary queen, and helped to translate the "Bishop's Bible." Edwyne Sandys was born at Hawkeshead, and his devotion to the culture of the young was rewarded in his son George, called by Dryden "the ingenious and learned Sandys, the best versifier of the former age." George was also an accomplished traveller, and wrote a good book about the East. The ancient seal of the "Grammar School" represented a master with a boy before him; the master's left hand points upward, his right grasps a bundle of birch rods. The motto is, *Docendo discimus.* Mr. Baines has learned enough by teaching to allow the birch to remain an antiquarian feature of the school on its seal. Altogether this school-house, with its surrounding larches, and the swallows flitting around it, and the clustering memories, was a very pleasant object.

As we looked, a tall and aged gentle-

WORDSWORTH'S DESK.

man passed its door, supporting himself by a cane, whom one could almost imagine to be Wordsworth himself revisiting the scenes of his boyhood. He was presently followed by a quaintly dressed old lady. They were on their way to the church, which is on the hill in a field near by. I was eager to see the Hawkeshead church, remembering the little picture of it in the "Prelude":

"The snow-white church upon the hill
    Sits like a thronèd lady, sending out
    A gracious look all over her domain."

A "restoration" has changed this snow-white to stone-gray, but it has also added a very sweet chime of bells, which ring out solemnly on the clear air. Around this church sheep and lambs are grazing, even up to its doors. Its Norman character is preserved. The decorations inside

FOX HOW.

are rather too new and bright, consisting chiefly of colored frescoes framing texts. While I was there alone a man entered and pulled at the ropes which rang the bells; then this bell-ringer disappeared into a room beside him, and presently reappeared in his gown, and moved up the aisle. Bell-ringer and clergyman were one and the same. Seven persons came to hear him read the daily morning service.

Ann Tyson was the name of the woman in whose cottage Wordsworth boarded. The house remains unchanged, and the room where the young poet

> "so oft
> Had lain awake on summer nights to watch
> The moon in splendor couched among the leaves
> Of a tall ash, that near our cottage stood."

Of Ann he wrote,

> "The thoughts of gratitude shall fall like dew
> Upon thy grave, good creature."

"Fair seed-time had my soul," wrote Wordsworth of his life at Hawkeshead. Rambling in this neighborhood he felt the

> "first virgin passion of his soul
> Communing with this glorious universe."

It was on neighboring Esthwaite Water that occurred the famous skating scene described in the first book of the "Prelude."

Even then, amid the merry scene and the glad voices of the boys, for this boy

> "far distant hills
> Into the tumult sent an alien sound
> Of melancholy;"

and it would not have been Wordsworth had he not sometimes retired from the uproar into some silent bay "to cut across the reflex of a star." In his tenth year it was, and in this vale of Esthwaite, that he felt

> "Gleams like the flashings of a shield, the earth
> And common face of Nature spake to him
> Rememberable things."

Among the boys was a beloved minstrel (Robert Greenwood, afterward Senior Fellow of Trinity, Cambridge), who used to take his flute when they went to row. They used to leave him on an island rock and go off a little way to listen; and

> "while he blew his flute,
> Alone upon the rock—oh, then the calm
> And dead still water lay upon my mind
> Even with a weight of pleasure, and the sky,
> Never before so beautiful, sank down
> Into my heart, and held me like a dream!"

But it is also pleasant to know from the poet that there was a house in this vale where, during summer vacation,

40

"mid a throng
Of maids and youths, old men and matrons staid,
A medley of all tempers, he had passed
A night in dancing, gayety and mirth."

Wordsworth began writing poetry while at Hawkeshead school, and here partly composed the poem entitled "Lines left upon a seat on a Yew-tree which stands near the Lake of Esthwaite, on a desolate part of the Shore, commanding a beautiful Prospect." This yew has been cut down because of a popular belief that its leaves were poisonous, and injured the cattle.

One might pass a long time in this peaceful vale and village, with the "Prelude" for guide; but we must part. Our last thought may well be upon kindly William Taylor, Wordsworth's schoolmaster, buried in Cartwell church-yard, where the poet wrote:

"He loved the Poets, and, if now alive,
Would have loved me, as one not destitute
Of promise, nor belying the kind hope
That he had formed, when I, at his command,
Began to spin, with toil, my earliest songs."

Our next visit is to Fox How, long the residence of Dr. Arnold, and still occupied by his daughter. The name may seem curious, but it was given the place in ancient times. "How" is a frequent name in the Lake district; it is from O. N. *haugr*, a sepulchral mound. Sometimes the remains of a warrior have been found in the hills so called, but the word seems to have been applied to any mound-like hill. The home of the Arnolds is a beautiful place in itself, but made more so by the remembrance of the good work that has been done here. Here the *History of Rome* was written. Here also Arnold used to gather around him the young scholars who were children of his nurture. Since his death it has remained a hallowed spot for the sons of old Rugby. John Keble little knew what he was doing when he persuaded Arnold to take orders in the Church: he was laying the corner-stone of the Broad-Church. Along these walks, and from these far away over hill and dale, two friends used to walk whose lives and works are the filtrated expression of Dr. Arnold's real aim and work. These two were Matthew Arnold and Arthur Clough. Together they studied, thought, succeeded. Fellows of Oriel when there the reigning spirits were Newman, Pusey, and the other Tractarian leaders, they were brothers amid these scenes of nature, and sat together at the feet of the great poet of Rydal, who loved them. Sometimes, with other friends, they would form a reading party in some charming nook among the lakes. "I came to Fox How about three weeks ago

DR. ARNOLD.

to meet Matt," writes Clough from Patterdale, July 31, 1844, and goes on to describe their ways. "We began with—breakfast, 8; work, 9.30 to 2.30; bathe, dinner, walk, and tea, 2.30 to 9.30; work, 9.30 to 11. We now have revolutionized to the following constitution, as yet hardly advanced beyond paper: Breakfast, 8; work, 9.30 to 1.30; bathe, dinner, 1.30 to 3; work, 3 to 6; walk, *ad infinitum;* tea, ditto. M. has gone out fishing, when he ought properly to be working, it being nearly four o'clock, and to-day proceeding in theory according to Constitution No. 2. It has, however, come on to rain furiously; so Walrond, who is working sedulously at Herodotus, and I, who am writing to you, rejoice to think that he will get a good wetting." The following year Clough writes: "First of all, you will be glad to hear that Matt Arnold is elected Fellow of Oriel. This was done on Friday last, March 28, just thirty years after his father's election. Mrs. Arnold is, of course, well pleased, as also the venerable poet at Rydal, who has taken M. under his special protection. The beauties of Parson's Pleasure, where we were wont to bathe in the early morning, have been diminished by the unsightly erection, by filthy-lucre-loving speculators, of a bathing-house, and I have therefore deserted it."

than any of them, and could never get too much of walking over it. The most pathetic incident of modern literary history is the death, at forty-three, of Arthur Clough. What a freight of treasures sank into that Florentine grave! Though his

PARSON'S PLEASURE.

Clough was always the best swimmer of his party; and he had a curious way of climbing a mountain by throwing his body forward, almost horizontal, toward the slope, and with long strides got ahead quickly. His friends declare that he knew this region, to its minutest detail, better

body is buried there, his heart is enshrined in the undying love of those who knew him in England and in America. There never was a tenderer love than that which has raised in this beautiful country, where the beauty of nature and friendship evoked from his brain the unique poem "Bothie of Tober-na-Vuolich" (notwithstanding its Scotch frame), a monument to that fine genius. In the September of 1861 he was rambling with Tennyson in the Pyrenees —he seeking health, Tennyson revisiting the spots where he had wandered with Arthur Hallam thirty-one years before. In less than a month from the time they parted, this second of the Arthurs Tennyson loved was dead, and a quatrain from "In Memoriam" is inscribed on the Grasmere cenotaph:

> "Now thy brows are cold,
> We see thee as thou art, and know
> Thy likeness to the wise below,
> Thy kindred with the great of old."

Having an introduction to the family now occupying Rydal Mount, we were in no danger of making the mistake of Hawthorne, who passed some time peering about, admiring, and perhaps pilfering ivy leaves from a fictitious Rydal Mount. He discovered next day that his enthusiasm had been lavished on the abode of a respectable Quaker. The affluence of flowers and foliage, which made it seem to Hawthorne as if Wordsworth's poetry had manifested itself in flowers, shrubbery, and ivy, still makes the better part of Rydal Mount. As we passed from room to room, they were filled with the fragrance of flowers. The old walk along the grounds, where the poet had chanted every line of his works, reverently as if at his breviary in nature's cathedral, is still here. We moved beneath the same archway of trees, and sat in the bower at its end, which reminded me of those which Mr. Alcott used to build in the grounds of his friends at Concord. Here the young Emerson sat, and listened to the poet reciting his poems. And here, indeed, or on his beat between this and the house door, was the real study and library of Wordsworth. The bower is made of the branches of trees, and its only ornament is such as has climbed from the earth or been deposited from the air. He must have sat here gazing upon Rydal Water with its islets, and the hills with their shining raiment of cloud and cascade, until he was in a state of absorption, like a holy Hindoo yogi in his sacred grove, on whose lap the serpent unnoted casts its skin.

A lady who in her youth passed some time at Rydal Mount, the families being intimate, told me that when she saw the old man out in this or some other haunt of his, silent, motionless, gazing, he appeared like some natural object. The very homeliness of his face was its attraction, and in its furrows there were tanned patches that looked somewhat like lichens. But it was not only in external habit and look that Wordsworth was a true Brahmin: he had strangely repeated in spiritual history the mystical development of his far Aryan ancestors. There was much discussion, soon after the "Ode to Immortality" appeared, as to what the poet meant by his thanksgivings for "fallings from us, vanishings, blank misgivings of a creature moving about in worlds not realized." A professor at Oxford related to me that, being on a walk with Wordsworth, he asked him what he meant by those phrases. Whereupon the poet grasped the rail of a gate with both hands, and said: "I have again and again in my life been driven to grasp the nearest object, like this, in order to convince myself that the world is not an illusion. It has seemed falling away, vanishing, leaving me, as it were, in a world not realized."

We went by the way of Radical Reform to Grasmere. Dr. Arnold gave the three roads between Rydal and Grasmere their names: the highest, "Old Corruption"; the middle, "Bit-by-bit Reform"; the lowest and most level, "Radical Reform." Wordsworth and his sister Dorothy also added to these new *Pilgrim's-Progress* names, having called a spot "Point Rash Judgment." Wordsworth never liked "Radical Reform," whereby a fine carriage-road had been carried over a country he had known when it was wild (to him another word for picturesque). But this is a region where one could by no effort escape the picturesque. When first the eye rests upon Grasmere Water, and upon the hills and dales everywhere, it really stills conversation; one lapses into a hushed feeling, as if it were dream-land, and a loud word might break the spell. The Grasmere cottages, too, were so charming that I could understand the absoluteness with which Hawthorne said, "This little town of Grasmere seems to me as pretty a place as ever I met with in my life." And among these none is more charming than Dove Cottage. Here, at the close of the last century (December 21, 1799), Wordsworth and his sister came to dwell, in what had formerly been a public-house—The Dove and Olive-Bough. There, in 1807, De Quincey visited him. "I was," he wrote, "ushered up a little flight of stairs, fourteen in all, to a little

NAB SCARR, HARTLEY COLERIDGE'S HOME.

drawing-room, or whatever the reader chooses to call it. It was not fully seven feet six inches high, and in other respects pretty nearly of the same dimensions as the rustic hall below. There was, however, in a small recess, a library of perhaps 300 volumes, which seemed to consecrate the room as the poet's study and composing-room, and such it occasionally was. But far oftener he both studied, as I found, and composed, on the high-road."

De Quincey had travelled with the family of Coleridge (who himself could not then go) to Grasmere, and his picture of the family at Dove Cottage is delightful. While the young man of twenty-two stands trembling, the figure of the "tallish man" emerges to salute him with cordial welcome, and after him came the ladies. "The foremost, a tall young woman, with the most winning expression upon her features that I had ever beheld, made a slight courtesy, and advanced to me, presenting her hand with so frank an air that all embarrassment must have fled in a moment before the native goodness of her manner. This was Mrs. Wordsworth. She was now the mother of two children, a son and a daughter; and she furnished a remarkable proof of how possible it is for a woman neither handsome nor even comely, according to the rigor of criticism—nay, generally pronounced

very plain—to exercise all the practical power and fascination of beauty through the more compensatory charms of sweetness all but angelic, of simplicity the most entire, womanly self-respect, and purity of heart speaking through all her looks, acts, and movements. Immediately behind her moved a lady much shorter, much slighter, and perhaps in all other respects as different from her in personal characteristics as could have been wished for the most effective contrast. 'Her face was of Egyptian brown'—rarely in a woman of English birth had I seen a more determinate gypsy tan. The eyes were not soft, as Mrs. Wordsworth's, nor were they fierce or bold; but they were wild and startling, and hurried in their nature." But the portrait of Dorothy Wordsworth is too well known for me to make room for its full length. The world has shared in the vision of her busy, thrifty hands making ready the cottage which De Quincey is to enter as the Wordsworths leave it. Dorothy was the "Martha" of all that circle of dreamers, albeit not without that sympathy with the poet which led Wordsworth to attribute to her so much of the influence which humanized his poetry.

Then came Coleridge. The Wordsworths were now (1809–10) living at Allan Bank, a mile away, and De Quincey in

Dove Cottage. Coleridge lived for a long time at Allan Bank as a guest, otherwise fed by De Quincey's library.

The romance of Mignon is hardly more pathetically beautiful than that which passed in this vale at that time. De Quincey, heart hungry, found in little Kate Wordsworth all that divine beauty and sweetness which Nature was aiming at in her flowers, streamlets, and rosy dawns. To walk these grassy lanes, to watch the growth of her mind, to listen to her lyrical voice—this was his library, his study, his heaven. He had often known what it was to wander all night, cold and nearly starved, along the streets of London, huddling with the wretched of both sexes under any rude shelter from sleet and rain; he had touched, albeit morally unscathed, the very floor of the pit of poverty and every horror; little by little he had toiled upward, and the benediction of his life, the spirit of his dawn after the long black night, was little Kate, nestling in his heart, interpreting for him the meaning of the world in her unconscious grace and joyousness. At sunset on June 4, 1812, she went to bed in good health; at dawn she was dead. "Never," wrote her unhappy friend—"never from the foundations of those mighty hills was there so fierce a convulsion of grief as mastered my faculties on receiving that heart-shattering news." His visits were no longer to Allan Bank, but to the little grave. Many a night of frantic grief did De Quincey pass on that grave. Then she rose again for him, and as he walked the fields her form appeared, but always on the opposite side of the field. "Almost always she carried a basket on her head; and usually the first hint upon which the figure arose commenced in wild plants, such as tall ferns, or the purple flowers of the fox-glove; but whatever might be the colors of the forms, uniformly the same little full-formed figure arose, uniformly dressed in the little blue bed-gown and black skirt of Westmoreland, and uniformly with the air of advancing motion." When this after-glow of a beautiful life episode sank, up rose in its place the dark phantasm which lurked in the drug with which a weary heart and worn body sought to still their pain.

Here, too, was passed another life of alternating brilliancy and tragedy—that of Hartley Coleridge. But for the evil habit that preyed upon him he had been a great man. One of his friends has spoken of him as sometimes like the lofty column which the simoom raises in its mighty breath; the inspiration of great passion ceasing, there remained only the desert sand over which the serpent crawls. Poor Hartley waged unceasing war with his serpent, but never quite conquered it. The cottage where he lived, Nab Scarr, still attracts visitors. Wordsworth loved him. When he heard that Hartley was dead (January 6, 1849), he was profoundly moved. "The day following," writes Hartley's brother, "he walked over with me to Grasmere, to the church-yard—a plain inclosure of the olden time, surrounding the old village church, in which lay the remains of his wife's sister, his nephew, and his beloved daughter. Here, having desired the sexton to measure out the ground for his own and for Mrs. Wordsworth's grave, he bade him measure out the space of a third grave for my brother, immediately beyond. 'When I lifted up my eyes from my daughter's grave,' he exclaimed, 'he was standing there.....Keep the ground for us: we are old people, and it can not be for long.'"

WORDSWORTH'S SEAT, GRASMERE.

III.

WE had sat on the old seat beside the hazel-tree in the garden at Dove Cottage, where Wordsworth used to compose his poems; had heard from the present owner about the lady who has for many years come there annually to gather a Christmas rose and lay on the poet's grave; had recalled by imagination the scenes, sorrowful and beautiful, which have consecrated that village, beside whose ancient Wishing Gate innumerable hearts have looked forth to happy prospects—some to be overcast, some to be realized; and had remembered Wordsworth's lines at that gate, beginning,

"Hope rules a land forever green,"

and felt the charm of its ending—

"Yea, even the Stranger from afar,
Reclining on this moss-grown bar,
Unknowing and unknown,
The infection of the ground partakes,
Longing for his Beloved, who makes
All happiness her own."

And now all these memories, scenes, homes, and lanes pointed one way, led up to one point—the grave-yard. There they had all ended. From the prehistoric Wishing Gate, where the fairies were once invoked, the path is short in space, but a vast journey in time, to the portal of Grasmere church, on which is written, "Whosoever thou art that enterest this church, leave it not without one prayer to God for thyself, for those who minister, and for those who worship here."

It was about noon. The church was empty. I walked around it, and read the texts on the walls, on their scrolls upheld by cherubim; examined the ancient font; read the Wordsworth tablet, just over the Rydal Mount pew, and gazed upon his noble face, which, carved there in marble, is ever close before the eyes of the clergyman. While my fellow-pilgrim was making his sketches, I went up into the quaint oaken pulpit, and sat there surveying the solemn interior, where the arms of old knightly families mingled with the symbols of peace and charity to form a shrine for memorials of intellectual greatness.

Wordsworth has left us in "The Excursion" a charming picture of Grasmere church and its pastor. The wanderer, the solitary, and he rested here on their walk. They entered, and the interior is described. Yet the wise discourse of the pastor which he reports was not given in the church, but outside on an old wall beside the Rothay. It appears, however, that his family and friends could not recognize in him who uttered such elevated

Wordsworth was never suspected of humor by any one except Mrs. Hemans. He claimed to have made one joke. A man met him on the road, and asked, "Have you seen my wife pass this way?" The poet replied, "I assure you, my dear sir, that I was not before even acquainted

THE WISHING GATE.

discourse on nature and human life any preacher they had ever known about Grasmere. At the time when it was written the rector was in an insane asylum, and the only preacher was a curate named Rowlandson, notoriously inadequate to any such discourse. Wordsworth then explained that the pastor he had described was an ideal character, combined of various individuals, the sermon being his own.

with the fact that you had a wife." Perhaps when his friends had read about the pastor and the elevated discourse, and came to him asking how that could be, when the curate was dreary and the rector insane, Wordsworth in like manner said, "My dear friends, I didn't even know that you had a curate."

Not far from Grasmere is a high place called Dunmail Raise. It was here, at the boundary between Westmoreland and

ST. OSWALD'S CHURCH, GRASMERE.

Cumberland, that Edmund, the Saxon king, defeated Dunmail, the last King of Cumberland, anno 945. The eyes of Dunmail's two sons were put out; he was slain; his kingdom was added to that of Malcolm, King of Scotland. There is a large pile of stones over the grave of Dunmail, innumerable travellers from his extinct kingdom having followed the pious custom of adding a stone to his cairn. We added ours.

But while we rested there, it appeared to me that there were some analogies between Dunmail Raise and Rydal Mount, and the two kings with whom they are associated. James Russell Lowell has spoken of the realm of the poet as "Wordsworthshire." He did indeed create such a shire, but it is extinct with him. In place of the humble stones which mark the resting-place of the last King of Cumberland, the cairn of Wordsworth is piled high with polished praises, tributes of poets, memorials that make a fair literature in themselves. No other modern poet has awakened so reverent enthusiasm. Yet Wordsworth was the last monarch of a realm of thought that has forever passed away.

THE WORDSWORTH GRAVES, GRASMERE CHURCH-YARD.

DUNMAIL RAISE.

vived in contact with nature, and it was Wordsworth who taught them how to distill from the fair earth a healing balm more soothing than the opium with which some of them had tried to still their heart-pains. Some passed a lifetime in being healed, but others grew strong while yet in their prime, and these found that the great life could not be lived in Wordsworth's mountain-and-lake cure.

About fifty years ago Carlyle and Emerson were walking together over the hills near Craigenputtoch; and then they sat down on a crag, and "looked down into Wordsworth's country." Such is Emerson's phrase, unconsciously significant. The two young men were, indeed, looking from a farther table-land of thought and purpose back upon the beautiful solitudes through which they had been guided by their spiritual fathers. They were destined to summon thought and poetry from that afternoon-land of bowers and reveries, and make them friends and leaders of humanity.

I am not sure but that this impression may be read upon the precious stone added to the wondrous cairn of Wordsworth by Matthew Arnold:

"Time may restore us, in his course,
Goethe's sage mind and Byron's force;
But when will Europe's latter hour
Again find Wordsworth's healing power?

"Keep fresh the grass upon his grave,
O Rotha, with thy living wave;
Sing him thy best, for few or none
Hear thy voice right, now he is gone."

That is a fine phrase and true, "Wordsworth's healing power." He came to a generation whose whole heart was faint. His own eyes had been seared by the French Revolution; he had returned from Paris to England with his enthusiasm for liberty chilled, and his hope for humanity nearly dead. A generation of thinkers was driven into reaction and solitude by the Revolution and the Napoleonic reaction that followed. These measurably re-

When Emerson was presently visiting Wordsworth, his admiration at the poet's "rare elevation" was followed by surprise at "the hard limits of his thought." Wordsworth had come to his "Raise": he could only a little understand Coleridge, thought Carlyle insane, and Goethe wicked; he had reached the boundary of his kingdom, which had to pass to Malcolm.

It is doubtful whether any thinker of equal culture will ever again feel a passion for the beauty of inanimate nature like that which Wordsworth felt, or so strangely repeat the emotions under which ancient nature-worship grew. The earth and air around him were so populous with the creations of his imagination, these being exalted to the stature of the exceptionally grand natural objects amid which he dwelt, that man and his affairs became petty, paltry, vulgar, in the presence of his majestic images. Yet, after all, a large part of nature is human nature. Wordsworth once invited Charles Dickens to visit him at Rydal Mount, praising the glories of that region. The novelist declined, and had something to say for the glories of London. "The wonder of these sights impels me into night walks about her crowded streets, and I often shed tears in the rustling Strand from fullness of joy at so much life. All these emotions must be strange to you: so are your rural emotions strange to me." Wordsworth was not without human sympathy and benevolence; it was his hope and aim to console, to bless, to uplift, and encourage hearts and minds; but he thought of these as individuals undergoing the checkered experiences of existence; the conception of universal humanity, progressive, triumphant, was a blossoming plant which the French Revolution tore by the root from his heart and brain. A primrose by the river's brim could give him more tears in his old age than anything that concerned the masses of mankind.

One need not therefore mourn that Wordsworth's cairn marks an extinct Wordsworthshire, while he rejoices that such a pure and saintly mind and character brought the chrism for the generation in which we live, by which it is consecrated to truth and virtue.

> "He found us when the age had bound
> Our souls in its benumbing round;
> He spoke, and loosed our hearts in tears.
> He laid us, as we lay at birth,
> On the cool, flowery lap of earth;
> Smiles broke from us, and we had ease;
> The hills were round us, and the breeze
> Went o'er the sun-lit fields again;
> Our foreheads felt the wind and rain;
> Our youth returned; for there was shed
> On spirits that had long been dead,
> Spirits dried up, and closely furl'd,
> The freshness of the early world."

Beautiful and polished as Rothay can smooth them be the stones laid on Wordsworth's cairn; white, too, as purified in Truth's well! So add I mine, small though it be, with reverence and gratitude; and so journey onward.

There are tempting by-ways all around us here; heights, vales, streams, not only picturesque in themselves, but from behind which rise shades noble or curious, faces that hold us with their glittering eye, and will tell us their story. They are so many that I am reminded of the rustic Cumberlander who bore along this road the specimens collected by a geologist. He found them heavy, emptied them

on the road-side, and refilled the bag from the turnpike when he came near Keswick, where the geologist anxiously awaited him. Even the carefully selected anecdotes and traditions of this region laid on the patient shoulders of *Harper's Magazine* would be more than a collector could hope to see again. We must barely glance once more at brave Robert

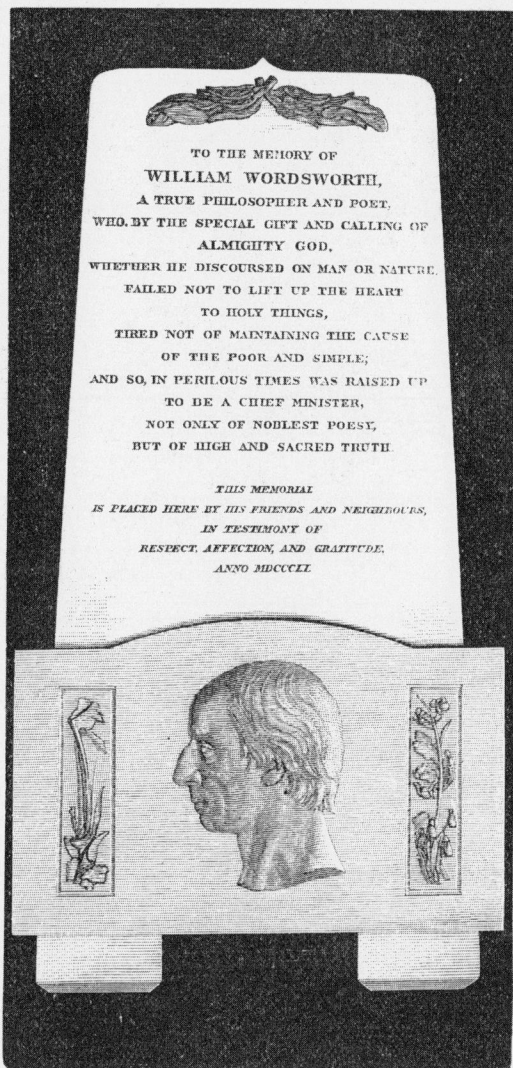

WORDSWORTH'S MEMORIAL TABLET, ST. OSWALD'S.

Walker, who near by entered upon his Leathwaite living, worth £50 a year, with a cottage, married a wife with £40, reared and educated eight children, and though his curacy never exceeded £50 per annum, left at the end of his sixty years' work £2000, and an imperishable memory for his charities. We must even pass by the Haunted House of Armboth Fells, where wide-eyed peasants see a large dog swim-

HELVELLYN AND THIRLMERE.

ming Thirlmere, welcomed by moving lights and ringing bells, and hear preparations made for a murdered bride, who still keeps there her ghostly nuptials. We can only nod to Lord Clifford, of Threkeld, who never learned to read or write, was for twenty-four years a shepherd boy, yet learned so much astronomy that he brought a noble fame to his estates when he came to them.

Next to the greatness of Wordsworth comes the grandeur of Helvellyn. The second mountain of England in height, it is the most impressive in appearance, and one does not wonder that it was the Holy Hill of the first inhabitants of this region. Ferguson thinks it was anciently El-Velin, that is, the Hill of Veli, or Baal. This mountain was one of the "high places" on which flamed the sacred fires, whose successors still light up some nooks and corners of this region. It is probable, however, that their name, "Baal-fires," or "Bel-fires," represents a Christian denunciation of them. It is possible still to find country folk who drive diseased cattle through the fire; and Miss Martineau found an instance where a considerate farmer, having driven his stock through a need fire, made his wife pass through also, she being as valuable as his ox or his ass. Many are the traces of ancient religion left in the names of this region; e. g., Rissen Scar (that is, the Giant's Steep); Scratch Meal Scar (Skratti being the Norse demon, our Old Scratch, and Mella being a female of the same character); Glenderaterra (valley of the demon of execution). Thirlmere (which Robert Ferguson, M.P., of Carlisle, a learned explorer of these subjects, believes was originally Thorolfsmere) breaks upon the sight beyond Helvellyn, and mirrors a long range of lofty steeps and crags—Fisher Crag, Raven Crag—so wonderful that we need not wonder that the Lake poets make this their trysting-place.

"The Rock of Names," midway between Keswick and Rydal, bears the initials of some of those who met there: W. W.; M. H. (Mary Hutchinson); D. W. (Dorothy Wordsworth); S. T. C. (Coleridge); J. W. (John Wordsworth); S. H. (Sarah Hutchinson). Wordsworth has described how they cut their initials, and the rock is still fulfilling his request:

"Fail not thou, loved Rock, to keep
Thy charge when we are laid asleep."

Beyond this region, awful in its grandeur, and so invested with names and traditions of that stern Scandinavian worship of the elements which made the pedestal for Wordsworth's adoration, we pass Castle Rock, the fairy castle of Scott's "Bridal of Triermain;" we visit "Wytheburn City," which has three or four houses and its church, which will just seat its score of citizens; then we emerge from the ancient world as our eyes look though the vale of St. John to the Christian spires of Keswick.

It is interesting to remember that the holy fires which lit up these hills

LOWER RYDAL FALLS.

in pagan times were continued in Christian times as St. John fires — they are still, wherever kindled, seen on St. John's Eve — and this vale has in it a remarkable circle of the kind called "Druidic," the name being only a term for our ignorance of their meaning. The original solar meaning may linger on "St. Sunday's Crag," as a peak is now called. As we skirt St. John's Vale, and draw near to Keswick, we find

WYTHEBURN CHURCH.

53

a large assembly gathered in and around a tent. It was a revival meeting got up by the evangelical clergy of Keswick and the adjoining region. Hymn-books were sold at the entrance; a luncheon was spread for strangers; and I was told that for some days there had been services and preaching from early morning to late in

eminent physician here. I also had the pleasure of here getting hold of his new book, *The English Lake District as Interpreted in the Poems of Wordsworth*. This little work came out rather too late to aid us in our tour through "Wordsworthshire" proper; but I have revisited the scenes in memory, with the professor

BRIDGE IN ST. JOHN'S VALE.

the evening. It was the nearest thing I had seen in England to an American camp-meeting, but it was conducted exclusively by clergy of the Established Church, aided by an eminent preacher from Switzerland. At Keswick we had the pleasure of meeting and walking with Professor Knight, of St. Andrews University, in Scotland, whose brother is an

and his poet for guides, and am amazed at the amount of work which the book represents. There is but one Wordsworth, and Knight is his prophet. Professor Estlin Carpenter is at Leathes Cottage, near this, and when we were there was engaged with the last pages of his biography of his aunt, Mary Carpenter.

Keswick is the most important town in

the Lakes; so busy, modern, respectable, that I felt a little chilled after coming out of the dreamy land of Grasmere. It is the very place one would associate with Southey, its most famous resident, who came to reside at Greta Hall after he had buried the dreams of his youth. For that matter it might be said that Wordsworth had buried his too; but no, his were slain in the streets of Paris at the Revolution, and when he came back he revived them all in an interior world, where no violence could reach them. It is now pretty well understood that Robert Browning's "Lost Leader" was an idealized portrait of Wordsworth, and it reports accurately the general feeling about him at the time it was written. But Wordsworth felt that this impression was not true.

Derwentwater.

I have heard that he never was known to be in a rage, except when hearing that some one (not Browning) had described him as reactionary. "Tell him he lies," thundered Wordsworth. This inward conviction that he was himself misjudged led him to defend Southey jealously from similar charges. Thomas Cooper, author of *The Purgatory of Suicides*, who was imprisoned as a Chartist, and from being a radical is now an orthodox preacher, visited Wordsworth in 1846. The laureate received him kindly at Rydal Mount, and said: "You were quite right; there is nothing unreasonable in your Charter. It is the foolish attempt at physical force for which many of you have been blamable." He warmly defended Southey from the charge of having been influenced by corrupt motives in changing his political opinions. Poor Southey had then recently died.

Samuel Taylor Coleridge preceded Southey at Greta Hall, and was the man who induced him to come. "Our house," wrote Coleridge (1801), "stands on a low hill, the whole front of which is one field and an enormous garden, nine-tenths of which is a nursery garden. Behind the house is an orchard, and a small wood on a steep slope, at the foot of which flows the river Greta, which winds round, and catches the evening lights in front of the house. In front we have a giants' camp —an encamped army of tent-like mountains, which, by an inverted arch, gives a view of another vale. On our right the lovely vale and the wedge-shaped lake of Bassenthwaite; and on our left Derwentwater and Lodore full in view, and the fantastic mountains of Borrowdale. Behind us the massy Skiddaw, smooth, green, high, with two chasms, and a tentlike ridge in the larger. A fairer scene you have not seen in all your wanderings." Coleridge mentions that he has access to "the princely library of Sir Guilfred Lawson," a baronet now succeeded by Sir Wilfrid Lawson, M.P. for Carlisle, famous as the champion who

ter and Lodore under his guidance. It was a charming afternoon when we rowed in the path of Dr. Syntax on the same lake.

> "With curious eye and active scent
> I on the picturesque was bent."

BUTTERMERE.

gives King Alcohol so much trouble. Sir Wilfrid is the man who reflects most honor upon Cumberland: wealth and rank have not in the least brought any reaction to that natural nobleman, whose presence, when he rises in the House of Commons, commands admiration from even those who wince under his sharp thrusts, and whose wit makes even the legislative brewers and victuallers laugh, while the fine-fledged arrows make them look like piteous Sebastians.

The other member of Parliament from this region is Robert Ferguson, of Carlisle, a gentleman who has written the best works on Cumberland, its antiquities and dialect. I had the good fortune to make the acquaintance of Derwentwa-

There is an island in Derwentwater which appears occasionally—some say periodically—on the water, varying in different years from an acre to a few perches. It emerges near Lodore, floats about, and some fine day retires under water. It vindicates Munchausen. There is a floating island in Esthwaite Water also, but it never disappears. It is only twenty-four yards by five, covered with alders and willows, and when the wind is high moves about like a fairy barge.

The regular islands in Derwentwater are beautiful, and of legendary interest. Lord's Island had an old building, from which was taken a clock bell, now that of Keswick town-hall; it bears the inscription, "H. D. R. O. 1001." The pleasantest

YEWS OF BORROWDALE.

island is that called "St. Hubert's": the same is mentioned in Rogers's "Pleasures of Memory"—

"Down St. Hubert's consecrated grove,
  Whence burst the consecrated hymn, the tapered rite
  Aroused the fisher's solitary night."

The people here have changed the name to St. Herbert. It is the name of a disciple of St. Cuthbert's, who is said to have lived here as a hermit. He prayed that he might not outlive his holy master, and at the moment when St. Cuthbert died at Carlisle, anno 687, it is said that Hubert was also found dead in this island.

Lodore is beautiful in the distance, seen from a point near Keswick, a pure white feather, which an assisted eye may see gently waving, like something alive, amid the dark green ravine. As we approach from the water we lose sight of it, but presently on the soft air we hear its voice,

HONISTON CRAG AND VALE.

gentle, harp-like; nearer, and its tone becomes solemn, organ-like; on shore, approaching, the tone rises through all the scale to a roar; and looking up the ravine one sees that the fall has hewn its own mighty instrument of sound. It is rare that one finds a fall where the phenomena of natural rhythm are so charmingly recognized, and they find fair interpretation in Southey's famous lyric on Lodore.

One morning the Abbé and I drove around by the east of Derwentwater, on a road carpeted with leaf-shadows and sunbeams, and passed down deep vales and over gentle hills, finding so much and such varied beauty that we felt as if one could never reach an end of it. At the Borrowdale Hotel they keep that well-known book in which tourists write their impressions. On one of the pages I read the following satirical verses:

"Strange Book, you prove a man may be
    A genius, and not know it:
My good friend Brown writes prose in town,
    But here he shines as poet.

"When he meets nature face to face,
    In verse he needs must greet her;
And if the chops be fairly cooked,
Here shall that vital fact be booked,
    In rather limping metre.

"And if the beds be duly aired,
    The tourist world shall know it;
And if posterity should care
    To know if it be—"

Alas! just here an incoming "Brown" requires the register, and my reader must supply the rest. But I have some sympathy for Brown. I can understand how he should aspire to sing his emotions as once a year he meanders, wanders, glides, at his own sweet will, amid these scenes. I have just met Brown sitting on the Bowder Stone, thirty-six feet high; he peeped over the Abbé's shoulder while he was sketching the Grange, then winked at Mary Anne, who was with him; and although I can not say as much for him as for those fine Oxonians and Cantabs we met at Grasmere and Coniston, yet Brown has the right stuff in him when he appends doggerel to his name in the register. A mole might become enthusiastic in sight of these ever-varying hills, their many-tinted sides and summits mirrored in their lakes—wonderful! wonderful! My pen falters, and must throw upon the faithful pencil of the Abbé the task of celebrating the Castle Crag, the wild Honiston Crag, and the majestic sweep of Buttermere.

58

I often find myself, however, after gazing upon these sublime things, longing for a scene more quiet, some "unpretending commonplace of nature." At the same time the least pretending thing that meets the eye here would be a nine days' wonder to one familiar with the gentle meadows through which the Thames winds its way near London town.

Perhaps as pleasing an hour as any we passed was at the Borrowdale Yews. Some philologers say that *yew* is radically the same word as *ever*; and these four trees might bear the name not only by their unfading green, but by the length of their years. It is awful to think of the age of these yews, beneath which Wordsworth imagined "ghastly shapes" holding their festivities or rites, while Darwin would probably think of them as housing the first arboreal men. Seated here on a mossy stone, turning our eyes away from the scarred summits of the hills, lulled by the four gentle rivulets which sing their way down past the yews to the full stream below, watching the butterflies, the creeping things, the luminous wild flowers, all joyful in the sunshine, we reflect how many generations of such animated beings—nay, of men like the poets who have celebrated them, and drawn others to seek them—have these great yews seen. They have borne no marketable fruit to man: they are not utilitarians; their trunks are gnarled, and one is a hut in which three may sit; but they bid fair to enjoy a green old age after the Victorian age shall have become as classic as the Elizabethan. One of them has lately been struck by lightning, as if Zeus had become jealous of his longevity; and though he was yet green, it may be that it is only like the vaunt of

GIANT'S GRAVE IN CHURCH-YARD, PENRITH.

LONG MEG AND HER DAUGHTERS.

some ancient institution which makes a transient show of life after its death-touch. One thing that impressed me was the way in which the aged trunks leaned toward each other and mingled their branches, like old friends left alone, on that bare slope of a desolate hill. Yet so gnarled and hollowed are their trunks, so ugly some of their lower dead branches, and so hewn and hacked are they with the names of Brown, Jones, and Robinson, that I fancy the gentle sigh I hear passing along their commingling needles is a longing for death.

They must have seen enough of life. When prehistoric man set up those "Druid" stones in St. John's Vale, they might have smiled upon his infant superstitions. They would have sheltered the Wandering Jew, had he come in this hol-low where I sit and think of Shelley's lines about him:

" Thus have I stood, through a wild waste of years,
  Struggling with whirlwinds of mad agony,
  Yet peaceful and serene and self-enshrined.
  Even as a giant oak, which heaven's fierce flame
  Had scathed in the wilderness, to stand
  A monument of fadeless ruin there;
  Yet peacefully and movelessly it braves
  The midnight conflict of the wintry storm,
      As in the sunlight's calm it spreads
      Its worn and withered arms on high
  To meet the quiet of a summer's noon."

It may have been that from sheltering many a wanderer in that mythical era these ancient trees gave their whispered secrets to Shelley while those lines were born in him. For hither, indeed, did he bring his girl-wife Harriet when they had eloped. Expelled Oxford for heresy in March, Shelley has eloped and married in September, and by October is dwelling at Keswick, since the only friend he now has in the world—a Duke of Norfolk—lives in this region. Protestant Oxford and orthodox parents have sent him forth into the world at nineteen an outcast; but a Roman Catholic duke stands by him, and this ancient temple of the Yews will raise heavenward arches above his excommunicated head. Harriet also was an exile; she had thrown "herself on his protection" from her father's petty tyranny.

EAMONT BRIDGE, ON THE BORDER BETWEEN WESTMORELAND AND CUMBERLAND.

ULLSWATER.

What mere children they were appears in a little story told by De Quincey. There was a pretty garden attached to the house near Keswick. They occupied only half the house, however, and when the Southeys called they asked Mrs. Shelley if the garden belonged to their part. "Oh no," she replied; "but then, you know, the people let us run about in it whenever Percy and I are tired of sitting in the house."

Southey was the only one who called upon them. De Quincey came, but the fledgelings were fled. Coleridge always regretted that he had not got hold of Shelley during that visit. "Why didn't he come to me? I would have understood him." It was but a brief butterfly existence they passed here. A few years later, and she was at the bottom of the Serpentine Water in Hyde Park; a few years more, and his form is undergoing with horrible literalness the water and fire which made the ordeal of life; and the only part of their united lives which one may recall without sorrow was that in which they "ran about" the Keswick garden, or skimmed Derwentwater, or, it may be, nestled in the covert of this ancient yew, and told fairy tales, or dreamed of a fair world never to be realized.

At Penrith we called on the venerable Orientalist Dr. Nicholson, one who, like many learned scholars to be found in England (more rarely elsewhere), with scholarship enough to stock several reputations, carries on his studies in seclusion. He told us much of the antiquities in the neighborhood. We then walked about under a grand harvest-moon; under its mystical light looked upon Penrith Castle, upon the picturesque old church, and the giant's grave beside it. That strange old monument so fascinated Sir Walter Scott that he would never pass through Penrith without stopping to gaze upon it. Eighty-four years ago Mrs. Ratcliffe travelled through this region, visiting the old castles and legendary places, which were the natural food of her mystery-loving fancy, and she also was much impressed by these runic stones, curiously carved, which stand like head-and-foot stones of a grave, but fifteen feet apart. "We pored intently over these traces, though certainly without the hope of discovering anything not known to the eminent antiquarians who have confessed their ignorance concerning the origin of them." So she wrote. The antiquarians have since "guessed" that it is the grave of Owen Cæsarius, once King of Cumberland, in which case it would seem to denote the size he assumed in popular imagination after his death. But it is a curious indication of popular feeling about the dead that this prehistoric tomb has remained as secure from exploration as that of the other giant who lies beside the Avon.

This is, perhaps, the richest region in antiquities of any in England. Next to

MAYBURGH MOUND; ARTHUR'S SEAT.

some pretty outlooks. In the centre is a large ash-tree, which has shaped its trunk to a stone twelve feet high, and curved at the top. Robert Ferguson of Carlisle believes that these circles were used for the *holmegang*, or "duel" of the North-men. This duel was a fair one, the swords being of equal length; but it was superseded by the Norwegian "duel of the girdle" (practiced up to the last century), in which the longest blade went to the strongest arm, each man, before commencing, sticking his knife into a block of wood, that part of the blade not buried being bound round with leather. The combatants were kept from running away by being buckled together by a girdle around their waists. Yes, it is well enough these old places should be silent. They are close to the river (Eamont) boundary between Westmoreland and Cumberland; and if, as is probable, they were places for executions and duels between the hostile kingdoms, we may turn from them to dwell with satisfaction on a signboard near Eamont Bridge, representing a Westmoreland and a Cumberland man shaking hands. Beneath the sign quite as many of them as is desirable now pass to take "a cup of kindness" together. Indeed, I suspect that the famous cup called the "Luck of Eden Hall," near this, the subject of Uhland's poem, is one in which the last rivals of this Border may have

Stonehenge, the largest of the stone circles is that a few miles out of Penrith, called "Long Meg and her Daughters." This consists of seventy-six upright stones, the largest, Long Meg, being fifteen feet in girth and eighteen feet in height. "Speak, giant mother," exclaimed Wordsworth:

"Tell it to the morn,
Whilst she dispels the cumbrous shades of night;
Let the moon hear, while emerging from a cloud,
At whose behest up rose on British ground
That sisterhood in hieroglyphic round."

But Long Meg does not speak through any letter or scratch on her side. Perhaps it is as well she does not. I have heard that an English traveller among the Tartars found a stone circle very much like this, with a large assembly praying in it. They went around from stone to stone, and prayed each to assist their cattle and crops, and said, "May our cows bring forth two calves at a birth, and may we sell them for double as much as they are worth." If Long Meg should ever have heard such prayers, she had better keep it to herself, and with her daughters remain a rosary of mystery rather than of superstition and selfishness. On our way we stopped to visit "King Arthur's Round Table," which is a large circle, such as one may conceive made by a basin fifty yards in diameter, pressed down, bottom uppermost, and so moulding the earth—this overgrown with long grass. And a few hundred yards from this is "Mayburgh Mound." This is a circle a hundred yards in diameter, surrounded by piled stones, among which grow ash-trees, through which are

BROUGHAM CASTLE.

pledged each other. The guide-books say the cup has on it the letters "I. H. S." This is not true; the letters are I. H. C. It is a beautiful cup, with ornamentation of red flowers and arabesque scroll on a blue ground. It is Oriental. The story is that a festive group of fairies, surprised by a servant at the well, left this cup be-ing together in peace and friendship to win sustenance from the earth. The hay-makers have a happy, substantial look, which one can hardly imagine to have been possessed by the old Border roughs and ruffians who preceded them. They do not seem to know anything of the eight-hour movement here. In harvest-

THE HAYMAKERS.

hind as they fled. One of them returned to get it, but finding it in the servant's hand, exclaimed as she flew away:

"If that glass should break or fall,
Farewell the luck of Eden Hall."

The cup is kept with great care. The prosaic-looking house ("Eden" here only means "the confluence of rivers") was the ancient seat of the Musgraves, and is still owned by Sir George Musgrave, baronet. From being chief of a Border clan the family came to give the king his chief in the Parliamentary war, and one so appears in the "Legend of Montrose"; so the family has been lucky enough to keep its name and estates.

We are in a region where, from the silent Druid graves to the grand castles—Brougham, Penrith, Lowther castles—everything tells of ancient struggles. And it is pleasant amid these battlements to see better crops than usual (for a deluged season), and laborers of both counties toil-

time they work twelve hours per day. They breakfast at six o'clock on oatmeal porridge, and sometimes coffee, with ryeleäf (rye loaf) black as a coal, and Dutch cheese. They "bait" (lunch) at half past nine, on ryeleäf, cheese, and beer. They dine at twelve on meat, potatoes, dumplings, and preserves. They take tea at four—bread and butter. They sup from nine to ten, supper being of much the same as breakfast. They are as hardy and quiet a set of folk as ever sprung from a restless race of fighters.

From Penrith a pleasant drive brings us to Ullswater, which means "Wolf's Water." Ulf was the first baron of Greystock, or Greystoke, now owned by the Howards, and the finest castle on this lake. The Norman form of the name was "l'Ulf," the Wolf, and it is preserved in Lyulph's Tower, a castellated shooting-box beside the water, built by the late Duke of Norfolk, Shelley's friend. Near it is the cascade called Airey Force. This glen is the scene of the somnambulist tragedy told by Wordsworth, in which Sir Eglamore returns from afar only in time to find his disconsolate Emma perishing in this torrent. She only lives long enough to discover his previously doubted constancy.

From Patterdale, at the foot of the lake, there is a glorious drive—provided tourists are weather-proof like those stalwart Oxonians who had here their favorite haunt, and do not limit their vision, like one party we saw, to the vault of their umbrellas—to the summit-house, the highest residence in the district, on the road to Ambleside. A man on our stage-coach manages to draw the attention of half our party from a landscape they had come a hundred miles, perhaps, to see, to an unextracted bullet in his arm, received from the Zulus. This bullet becomes the seed out of which grows an Igdrasil of political discussion. It is possible that Wordsworth had known much of this sort of thing before he wrote those lines, found *passim* in his poems which show how petty a creature man commonly is in the presence of nature's grandeurs.

But this small bullet and the small-talk over it remind us that we are on our way into the world of affairs again. Hark! is that the nightingale? No; it is the steam-whistle! Our revels now are ended. The steam-whistle startles the air, and sends the mountain spirits back to their ravines and caves again. The Genii of the Lakes protested against this form in which Triton came to blow his wreathed horn on Windermere. Wordsworth placed across the railway track a sonnet that seemed insurmountable, but it came on nevertheless; and on the whole we find it comfortable that we can take a good look at Windermere and the mountains in the morning, and talk them over at our London dinner-table the same evening. Nevertheless, they who would see the English Lakes as they environed the Lake Poets, who would know something of their sweet solitudes and their simple-hearted peasantry, would act wisely in embracing the earliest opportunity to visit them. They will no doubt be able to do it very rapidly and cheaply ere long, but whether it will be so well worth doing may be doubted.

THE LUCK OF EDEN HALL.